I0816797

A Dedication to Beauty

A Dedication to Beauty

An antiquarian's life with antiques and old houses

MEL SHAKESPEARE

FIREFLY BOOKS

Published by Firefly Books Ltd. 2025

First printing

Library of Congress Control Number: 2025934885

Library and Archives Canada Cataloguing in Publication
Title: A dedication to beauty : an antiquarian's life with antiques and old houses / Mel Shakespeare.
Names: Shakespeare, Mel, author.
Description: Previously published: Cobourg, Ontario: Songbard Press, 2024.
Identifiers: Canadiana 20250173883 | ISBN 9780228105923 (hardcover)
Subjects: LCSH: Dwellings—Conservation and restoration—Ontario. | LCSH: Historic buildings—Conservation and restoration—Ontario. | LCSH: Dwellings—Conservation and restoration—Ontario—Pictorial works. | LCSH: Historic buildings—Conservation and restoration—Ontario—Pictorial works. | LCSH: Shakespeare, Mel. | LCSH: Antiquarians—Ontario—Biography.
Classification: LCC NA7242.O5 S53 2025 | DDC 728/.37209713—dc23

Published in the United States by
Firefly Books (U.S.) Inc.
P.O. Box 1338, Ellicott Station
Buffalo, New York 14205

Published in Canada by
Firefly Books Ltd.
50 Staples Avenue, Unit 1
Richmond Hill, Ontario L4B 0A7

Photo Credits
James A. Chambers: 32, 33, 35, 36; Keith Marlowe: 187;
Sally Hood-Ranscombe: 144, 148; Don Proctor: 200, 201, 205;
Roger Brooks: 216–223

Printed in China | E

We gratefully acknowledge the financial support of the Government of Canada for our publishing program.

For the mother I never knew.

"What ever is good in it's kinde
ought to be preserv'd in respect to antiquity,
as well as our present advantage,
for destruction can be profitable to none
but such as live by it."

Nicholas Hawksmoor,
in his explanation of designs for
All Souls College, Oxford 1715

Contents

10 *Introduction*

16 Saved from the burn pile
28 A bit of Quebec in Ontario
38 Peace in the valley
48 Twenty years a slave
62 The piece-sur-piece surprise
70 The Great Pretender
84 The coop de ville
92 A journey back to the past
102 Two centuries later
114 In good hands
130 What lies beneath?
142 The house of six Sallys
158 A legacy born to live

168 The seven-bay beauty
180 The church on the hill
188 Meant for each other
198 Built before Fort York
206 The silk purse
216 The coast-to-coast cape
224 A bachelor's cozy den of log
230 Still reaching for the sky
236 The ultimate antique
244 Majestic over Milton
254 The art of craft and the craft of art
264 You've reached Whitsend
276 The homeless collector

Introduction

There is a timeless truth that is as relevant today as ever — and that is tradition. To speak of tradition is to speak of an immutable principle and an idea that transcends this moment by its having been a primary precedent of conscientious men.

Tradition, not as custom or habit, nor even as the transient style of a passing age, but tradition as the guiding principle by which men carry continuity of their most essential and useful forms with them. This presiding idea animates society, determines what man makes, how he makes it and fashions life to the point of art — if he is steadfast in his principle and remains cognizant of his spiritual self. By doing so, he surrounds himself with forms that echo transcendent archetypes using fundamentals not founded by his forebears but maintained by them. This is the window to his soul and the cornerstone whereon his love is laid.

"Every beauty and greatness in this world is created by a single thought or emotion inside a man. Everything we see today, made by past generations, was, before its appearance, a thought in the mind of a man or an impulse in the heart of a woman." — Kahil Gibran

And it is the product of these thoughts that have inspired us, and continue to inspire us, that have become valued form, that help us align and create our present, that allow a spiritualizing of the emotions subtle and refined, that let immortal beauty into the eyes of mortal men. In these days of cold facts, commercialism and expensive frontages, one feels that art is being shoved into the discard pile. And when a good building is demolished to make room for an "ultra-modern" duplex or coffee shop, one knows that the Goddess of Beauty is getting an awfully raw deal.

I suppose I'm a man of the past. I think I miss the 18th century, among others. I certainly resonate with the philosophy of those times when good taste was an achievement pridefully kept in mind and shown in the craftsmanship of homes and their interior furnishings. It was this that served and comforted homeowners every day.

As close as one may come to the days of yore is to collect those things we call antiques, having an eye of course to those that please us with their beautiful lines that show the honest application of someone's skill and care.

When I began to notice a certain incongruity that was showing up too often between the antiques themselves and the houses that contained them, I wondered if there might be a solution. I came to believe that the building of a house is not too removed from the building of a piece of furniture. Could this be the context that was required? An old house for those old antiques? It didn't seem so unreasonable to me. I decided to do just that for myself.

Those old log houses from the early 19th century were available in northern Ontario. True, most were in bad shape but not entirely. I thought I might find one worth restoring. A year later, there it was, the contents of our antique collection, standing up against the huge pine walls and strewn throughout this venerable house, looking like they were meant to be there all along. I knew then that I could dedicate my life to bringing this beauty to others as often as it was required of me. This was the first of many such projects I took on for others that had a similar thought. Each of these few homes I'm about to share with you, twenty-six out of many more, come with an inherent story that expresses the love of their custodians as well as the joy they gave to me upon building them.

In terms of "architecture," if what is being built today is mere construction and ceases to relate to the soil it stands upon, where are we to look for inspiration? So much of the arts of man have become mere decoration, with art's first function, having been sacrificed in the name of abstraction. In the multi-media world of advertising and hype, significant traditions suffer from technological applications common to a person's lower nature. Predominant today, the industrialization of buildings provides little more than boring skylines wherein we may safely toil. A modern person works too hard at life, somewhat cut off and segregated from their more natural contented self. A more natural ambition would be to express themselves with the beauty that is their birthright.

The advent of these times seldom brings more skill, and often less, to this matter. Where once the craftsperson specialized and maintained a high degree of excellence, work now lacks the stamp of good training and the soundness of careful, deliberate application. It was the persistence in fundamentals, instilled and instigated by the apprentice system, that prepared these creators to do good work. To this day there is still no better lesson than years of service in the presence of the masters who readily impart their craft and secrets to the novice willing to learn the blend of beam, panel and furniture to give a room character and distinction.

Sometimes we are fortunate to see the genius of the architect and skill of the builders who executed a work at their best. There were some spaces well-conceived but I found few of the attributes I required to be comfortable. I often found them devoid of feeling, uninviting and spiritless. If the same pride of craftsmanship and care that had fashioned the could the structure that contains them, harmony would be immediately evident and a no more welcome threshold could be imagined.

One of the first antiques I ever bought was a stuffed Peregrine falcon. I thought it was so beautiful, besides having the quintessential design to maintain its superiority in the air — the craft it was built for — killing. I admired it for a long time but it went the way of most of my things (not that I ever really owned them), sold or given to someone else who also appreciated them. Then there was a carving that seemed to mesmerize me. I think it must have been from Ceylon or somewhere in Indonesia. It had elephants and monkeys intricately interwoven into the blond jungle foliage. I suppose the wood was cedar, the whole piece being so light. What fascinated me was the realization of the genuine effort someone my this piece of art, for art it was.

I was about fifteen or so and was always finding new things, especially those that were old, to beautify my room. Actually, thinking back, I suppose the collecting bug first bit me when I was even younger, perhaps ten, when stamps became my passion. I had so many albums of beautiful stamps in all sizes, all colors and from so many countries. Maybe that instilled in me an interest in travel later but that's a side issue. It seemed there was no end to the stamps that would be carefully put in an order to be proud of. Then there were the Dinky toys; cars, trucks, military vehicles, trailers, etc. They came in all colors and in a wondrous small scale that seemed impossible at the time, the perfect toys for a youngster. I built little garages and outdoor tracks for them to travel on. That helped them come alive for me. I won't go into the chemistry set stage. Perhaps it was not so different for others so inclined, with its potential for explosions. Often, it seemed, there wasn't much left to keep afterward.

When I began art studies in my teens, I relished visits to the Royal Ontario Museum where I could find the various arts and crafts that showed off treasures of the world, their quality passed down for our study and appreciation. It was the first time I think, that I came to believe that the so-called "primitive" societies had it over us in their fabrications of expertly executed material, whether it be metal, wood, stone or any natural material for that matter. Their cultural education was handed down to them quite directly. They had the dedication not only to perpetuate it, but take it even further into realms of beauty.

In later travels through the world I always included visits to the best museums, whether in Hawaii, Japan, China or France, among others. A visit into the deep caves of Lascaux France to witness the Palaeolithic paintings on the stone walls left me gaping at the indelible fact of their ancient human history passed directly to me.

Yes, there are many things that can be collected but there is probably one thing that leads us to become collectors. I think it comes down to a development that is ongoing — the proper appreciation of the craftsmanship or handiwork of the generations that went before us. Certain pieces appear before us (if we have a diligent eye and the hunting urge) that exude a deliberate honesty — a piece that was fashioned with a quest for beauty. They become the items that come as close as possible to give meaning to a very personal effort. Then it comes alive in its own way to represent a particular moment in one's eternal spirit. That could be the raison d'etre for all collectors that aspire to a beautiful thing that becomes many things that take on a life of their own, a connection to an even larger beauty that you then devote yourself to preserve and take care of. Doesn't that also lead to a collection of collectors who also love beautiful things that sometime pass between them? These are the love objects that are handed down through the generations, not just for the beauty of them but for the soulful creativity that made them. And what better way to span the gap between the first hearthfire and the homemaker of today than surrounding oneself with beautiful creations that emit a charisma that adds dignity to life.

It may be this fact alone that led me to the longer, adventurous journey through my life that I hadn't expected. I hadn't realized at the time that it would have to do with creating an honest context for collectors. It is true that each single piece of wonderful furniture may stand alone, wearing its beauty proudly. But does it not look even more beautiful next to or surrounded by others like it? When I and my wife Jean moved from the city our first rental home was in Unionville, a common suburban brick bungalow built in the fifties. The start of our furniture collection, early 19th century Quebec pieces, I must say, did not seem to fit against those dull colorless walls. There was something to be done about that and we had to do it ourselves. We would move further out, to the country, and build something that suits us. We would do our best to create an environment to complement those things of beauty that we cherish. It couldn't be that daunting of a task.

It happened, as do all things one sets ones mind to, just outside Uxbridge, eight acres, a simple cottage (perhaps a "teardown"), a stream, a potential pond, a lot of work. We were young and determined — and lucky too, I guess. We had found a log house, just the thing, natural and old. We could easily envision our furniture set against those huge logs. We'll add it to the cottage. It turned out it was the dream we'd share our life with. We didn't realize at the time that we were spoiled with this particular log house. The logs were so large that it only took six tiers of them to stand a story and a half high. We thought naively, that all log houses had logs this size.

A year later, I built a board and batten building that became the antique shop. Then a post and beam barn was needed for overflow. Antique collectors seemed to like our stuff. Maybe it was because I took what turned out to be a relatively new approach to collecting. I came to realize that the original colors that some pieces wore (sometimes under layers of paint and sometimes, if you were lucky, without an over-paint) were quite beautiful and should never be stripped. Once shown this straightforward method of restoration, a clientele of the same mind grew, enough to keep our shop flowing, providing I could keep finding the inventory.

Jean and I had a stroke of luck in 1966. We were on an extended European trip and belated honeymoon. We found a dealer of antiquities in Lucerne, Switzerland. He had six fantastic pieces of furniture that predated the kind of things we'd find at home by a century or two. We couldn't leave them behind. To keep the story short — we traded the pieces to a Swiss couple who had an antique shop in a converted church and a barn full of Canadiana furniture in the town of Kettleby, Ontario. The swap kept our shop full for years.

But that didn't stop the quest for more furniture. Further hunting took me far afield — through Ontario and Quebec to begin with. It took a while to learn the paths to good New England dealers. If you latched on to a dealer with honest old stuff they'd often tip you off to where you might discover the next great finds. Eventually you had a chain of dealers where you could always find something to add to the load. I'd point my Chevy Suburban home when I couldn't fit in one more thing, or perhaps I just ran out of purchase power. Fortunately, there were always collectors ready to help offload the new treasures when I arrived home. Of course the great finds often created a conundrum — what would furnish the house and what would furnish the shop?

Like the time I found the Louis XIV Quebec Buffet in a Pennsylvania barn and repatriated it back to Canada. It was perhaps the best piece I'd ever found. It was 1975 and the very first Bowmanville show was to commence in two weeks. We decided to take fewer items, offering the best quality we could. It sold to the first buyer in the room. I did eventually buy it back years later though. One thing I came to enjoy about picking in New England, the American collectors were ahead of us in collecting the best furniture we had in Canada. This was why I was able to bring back an exceptional piece on almost every load.

There were those collectors that came into the house to admire our own collection. That was when things changed considerably. A few couples fell in love with the log house, immediately realizing that was what they wanted as well. They asked if I would build one for them. I loved building ours and learned a lot about building while doing it. I thought why not? In my travels picking through Ontario I'd seen other log buildings with similar potential. Before I knew it, I was building a couple every year, usually for those who also needed the right home for their antiques.

It didn't take long to organize a crew of artisans who loved the work, as did I, taking down the good ones, restoring them and putting them back up, wherever they were needed. I started the business, Tradition Home Designs, a design/build business with me working basically as the architect and builder that took the projects to whatever stage was required. It took us all over North America, which we all found to be quite exciting. It turned out to be a lucrative career, the best part being the great friendships that were inevitable, having clients with the same sensibilities as ourselves, finally able to live in the home of their dreams.

I've had this idea for quite a while — putting some of my houses in a book, while telling the stories that go with each of them. I couldn't find a photographer that could travel all over the country, especially to some of the distant American states where some beauties that we'd built reside. Alas, I couldn't get to them either. They were adventures in themselves. So, I took it upon myself to use some of the best photographs I had hung on to from over the years, while taking more in the last few months. There are twenty-six houses shown here, just a portion of the bunch, but a book can only be so big. Each house is unique with the majority being of log construction, post and beam or stone. I hope you may enjoy and find each home of interest. It has been my pleasure to restore these homes, once considered derelict. I attempted to bring each alive again for wonderful new custodians to give them the love they deserve. And the friendships that occurred over the course — I couldn't count them.

— MS

NOTE: I am not known for my photography, and perhaps some of the photos tell why! I didn't have an iPhone way back when we started all this. Thank you iPhone for the help!

Saved from

the burn pile

Our first log house,
rescued in 1965,
totally spoiled us.
I thought all log houses
would have twenty-four
inch logs

preceding page
Table
Ontario, c. 1820, Pine sawbuck with original red base scrubbed top.
H 30" W 108" D 30"

Bowl
18th century, double-handled ash bowl Eastern Great Lakes.
L 22" W 16"

Chandelier
Gaspe, Quebec, late 18th century, eastern white cedar, original red, green and gold paint. Every candle lit at every New Year's party.
H 23" W 36"

After living in the city for a couple of years after we were married, Jean and I moved out to Unionville where we rented a small bungalow. We toyed with the idea of buying (make that mortgaging) a house in either Unionville or Markham but we really wanted a country property where we could possibly build our own house. I'd learned enough about building to give it a go.

We spent quite a few weekends driving around the country not realizing the price of vacant lots, even when quite a distance north of town. When we happened across an eight-acre lot near Uxbridge with a cottage for sale we were excited. It even had a clear stream meandering through it, which gave me the idea of an eventual pond. The cottage seemed to have a bit of soul, the owner being a well-known violinist. We agreed it was just right for us, just about everything we'd hoped to find.

The cottage definitely needed something though. I had in mind some ideas to renovate the place with more traditional lines, add a fireplace, some beamwork perhaps, but it was such a small place, certainly not fit or large enough for year-round living, and we now knew we wanted to live in the country. I knew I never did feel at home in the Big Stink. What to do? Could we really "trade city soot for sylvan charm" as advertised in one of my favorite movies, *Mr. Blandings Builds His Dream House?*

The cottage was about the size of a summer kitchen wing often found sprouting off the back of a typical mid-19th-century farmhouse, the abandoned kind I'd been sketching and poking around in for years. If I could just find one of those early log houses I've always admired to add on to this thing, that could do it. The character. The dimension. The drama.

Table
Quebec, c. 1830, scrubbed pine top, original brown paint, on birch frame and cabriole legs. Came off top of car coming back from Quebec, landed in tall grass, with no breakage.
H 28" W 34" D 24"

Chair
Quebec, c. 1800, country Capucine form, Original splint seat, remains of original red paint.
H 40" W 24" D 18"

Fact was, the more I thought about it, it was the perfect place to house all those early Canadian antiques that looked okay in our rented suburban bungalow but it was also poor context for them, to say the least. The narrow hardwood floors, tiny cramped rooms, the lack of a working fireplace, so many things shouted — get out! Maybe this was our chance to get out. It wasn't cheap though.

"Where would we ever get nineteen thousand dollars?" asked Jean. Of course that called for some very serious deliberation.

Well, the cowboy in me had a hobby. For the last few years I had been collecting antique Winchester rifles, working up to a small but select group of them. It seemed a good investment as well as a satisfying pastime. I had an idea that was worth a try. I called a collector friend who always coveted my seven high-end Winchesters that even included the rare Henry rifle, also in superb condition. It was a shorter call than I expected.

"Would you pay twenty for them?" I asked.

"Done." he answered. That was it. Our first property, bought and paid for. And no mortgage ... yet.

Well, the property had potential but we knew there'd be some real work ahead of us. The cottage was not very well built but at least it was enough to house us while we made some improvements. The heating system was ridiculous, coming from a small shack that was tacked onto the end of the building. The floors sagged quite a bit and had to be shored up from underneath. Because there was only one foot of clearance under the floor joists, needless to say, it was a filthy job. Oh, did I

Logs
An excited Jean shows off the 24" logs of our first house at Roseville, just outside of Uxbridge.

mention, it was a small cottage, basically three rooms; a tiny bathroom, a tiny bedroom and a communal kitchen cum dining room.

Then there were the grounds that were so over-grown that it was difficult to even get around the eight acres. If there was ever going to be a pond I might have my work cut out. We had to set some priorities. The idea of course was to add on to the cottage. I thought we needed a good size building on the north end. The cottage would then look like a later addition. It would be the main living room and possibly the master bedroom. I had an idea and fortunately, Jean liked the same idea ... an old log house, one of those early 19th century log houses that we've seen in the Ottawa Valley.

There began the hunt. I scoured just about every road up there, only finding poor examples of log houses left to the ravages of the harsh Canadian winters. After about a year we'd given up the idea.

One very wintry Saturday morning I was on my way out the door, off to the local lumberyard in Uxbridge to price the lumber for a stick-frame building when Jean told me to hold up. I came back in to read the small ad in the local paper. It was a log house for sale. I didn't recognize the phone exchange. It could have been from anywhere. Of course I called right then and there. To our surprise, it was in small hamlet just up the road. I told the seller I'd be right up, even though a snowstorm was raging. I met the fellow, who was a writer named Ian Adams, who lived in a restored log house of all things. He explained how he had just rescued it from the farmer who was about to put it in a pile to burn it. It seems he was ridding himself of this one-hundred-and-fifty-year-old heap to make room for his dream home — a brick bungalow like the one we couldn't wait to vacate. What a riot!

We went out back to observe a mountainous snowbank with one log sticking out. It was two feet wide. I asked him if they were all like that.

Armoire
Quebec, 18th century, with linen fold panels, multi layers of paint over two centuries.

Armoire (opposite page)
Astorville, Quebec, 18th century, Pine, diamond point doors, red stain then green paint found after later brown paint was removed with dull-edged spoon. Hours unestimated.
H 56" W 51" D 21"

He confirmed the fact and I asked the price. Two thousand seemed fair to me so I agreed to it. So I paid Mr. Adams, got the logs to the site, puzzled over the scratch of paper that tried to make sense of the order of log wall building and, after some confusion, began to erect these mammoth logs carved from Ontario's virgin forest. Or rather, "Tiny," the six-foot-six, two-hundred-and-fifty-pound crane operator erected them with some direction from the novice owner. Things clicked into place pretty well thanks to the brave and talented craftsmen who had hewn the logs with their tight-fitting dovetails so may years ago. If it didn't fit tight and plumb it was our best clue that we were hoisting the wrong log. The

Mat
Labrador, c. 1920, hand-hooked at Grenfell Mission. Graced our gray/blue seven drawer chest for years.
H 9" W 11"

granite cornerstones for the chimney were retrieved from nearby barn foundations and laid by a local stonemason. The fireplace with its bake oven and hearth I copied from the early 18th century "Indian House" in Deerfield Mass.

Soon we had roof decking, a set of period-style windows in place and a second floor loft. A few mistakes were made, of course. I chose hand-split cedar shakes for the roof and ended up shoveling them off a couple of years later, replacing them with sawn shingles. It was nice to keep the weather out. And when I contracted for the chinking between the logs I came home from work one day to find the interior of the logs partially covered with cement mortar. Not what I had in mind! Fortunately, I caught it in time before it set rock hard. A few days later we had scraped and cleaned back to the wonderful texture and color of wood.

In trying to find some history of the house one piece of information seemed to ring true, though to this day is unsubstantiated. Evidently, the survey crews delegated by General Brock to map the counties would erect a survey station every so many miles apart. The surveyors were also very skilled at building with the trees available. This particular house

used immense timbers the likes of which I had never seen till then and seldom since. It didn't appear to be something thrown up quickly by a farmer impatient for shelter.

Here we were with this great room 22 ft. by 30 ft. to furnish. It cried out for the good stuff. It seems our early stuff was the right stuff. The furnishings seemed to feel right at home at last. We did too. Many trips to those period villages both in Canada and the U.S. gave inspiration and ideas, not to mention they were buying trips too.

Hogscraper Candlesticks (left)
c. 1840
Exceptional 16" pair found at Roger Bacon's in the early 1970s.

So now Jean and I had to furnish the antique shop. Yes, the one we built at the end of the lawn. Not that you could call it lawn. We were, after all, chopping our place out of the woods like pioneers. The shop was for the spillage, those items we couldn't find room for in the house. Besides, it was fun to restore pieces and meet others who appreciated them as much as we did. Actually, we were sort of rebels in the game

Sawbuck Table (opposite page)
Waterloo, Ontario, pine top with partial blue/gray paint, hardwood base with solid blue/gray paint, possibly Mennonite.
H 30" W 120" D 36"

Coffeepot (opposite page)
New England tole, first half 18th century, bright red and yellow on black ground.
H 10.5" Base 6.5"

HutchTable
New England, c. 1830, pine scrubbed top with base in original old red paint.
H 30" Base 20" x 16", Top 36" diameter.

in that we very soon realized the mistake of stripping furniture and attempted to persuade clients to take the items home in their beautiful early colors. Nowadays, those pieces go for a Prime Minister's ransom. Well, maybe more than that.

Friends and visitors seemed to love the log house as much as we did. Next thing I knew I was persuaded to build something similar for a friend and his wife. They too wanted a more appropriate place for their antique collection. Well, one led to the next and it soon became another vocation with me and a couple of enthusiastic workmates traveling around Ontario salvaging, restoring and re-erecting period log homes on wonderful natural country sites.

And today, after so many years, my respect for our forefathers' strength and character never diminishes but only grows. I continue to build in the tradition that gave us the log home and always delight in finding the next one to pass on to those of like mind who have the desire for preservation, heritage and beauty. I didn't realize till many years later, after finding and building dozens of log houses, that this first one was the best one ever. We were spoiled.

After many happy years and fond memories of living in the log house, our first real home, we did move on, designing and building in their early forms. But that's another story. I cannot say however, that I've felt more comfortable or more at home in them than there in the woods by the stream in that house of logs.

Table
Quebec, 17th century, Louis XIII style with flame finial.

Dish Dresser (opposite page)
Found near Rockwood, Wellington County, Ontario, original gray/red paint, pegged construction, original hardware.
H 75" W 59.5" D 18"

A bit of Quebec

in Ontario

I needed an art studio and a place for Quebec antiques — mission accomplished!

If you were to look for Canada's earliest tradition other than the aboriginal you must start with the French architectural style. I've always been intrigued and beguiled by it, particularly the fieldstone cottages often whitewashed over with their multi-paned casements and colorful shutters. I think of the Habitants themselves, who have shown us their strength of character and perseverance to carry such a simple, bold form to a new land with faith and self-confidence. This architectural form, adapting itself to nature and its natural surroundings, water, land and forest, thus came to rest honestly and comfortably in its new Habitant environment. Of these people's water — I have some experience. In my more adventurous youth, favorite tales of the *coureur-de-bois* eventually led me into their wilderness. I'm sure I shot many of the same rapids they met up with centuries ago. The few homes I saw along the river trails always impressed me though at that time I had not thought architecture would become so much a part of my future.

It did occur to me at the time, however, that there was little else that could carry one back as far to the first days of colonization, and whose merit lies in their being of another age.

Blueprint (**above**)
Roseville, 1981, showing design elements required to reproduce an 18th century Habitant cottage.

L'Atelier (**right and opposite page top**)
Roseville, 1983, original door and storm door and lock, original 18th century casements and shutters. Stonework by Glen Ward.

Studio
(**opposite page, lower**)
Interior of cathedral style art studio with painted stone walls, heated stone floors and early Quebec furniture. An open studio for artist friends every Tuesday.

OPEN STUDIO | 20 YEARS

I used to travel extensively and I particularly remember one trip across the breadth of France where patient old houses stood for generations to watch us grow from barbarians to something somewhat more human. I came to understand that it is architecture that joins yesterday with tomorrow and the march of tradition must be guarded with a good heart and a definite will to do so.

With this appreciation in mind it did not seem so unusual for one man's folly to turn in a particular direction. I needed another building. A painting studio. A place for some of the best of the French Canadian antiques spilling out of the log house. Of course, what could be more appropriate than a Habitant cottage? I had a great spot in mind on the other side of the pond up against the hill. There was the stream however, tight up against that hill, so it might be a tough squeeze.

Buffet Bas
Quebec, first half 18th century, Louis XIV in original blue paint and forged iron hardware, repatriated from Pennsylvania in 1975.

Bonnetiere
Quebec, first half 18th century, original black paint baluster hinges, decorative escutcheons, beaded doors and part of our Port Neuf collection.
H 67" W 23" D 18.5"

Cupboard
Quebec, c. 1820,
Adam manner, pine,
imitation graining of
wood over original blue
paint, reeded chevrons,
dentil moulding,
Chippendale bracket feet,
replaced latches.
H 77" W 47" D 17"

I knew I had the manpower: a great stonemason and good carpenters. We just came off a large stone house reproduction so I knew we could meet the challenge. And we had rebuilt a French Canadian log house from Rimouski just the previous year. How could I free them up for a non-profit endeavor?

Well, not to worry. Let's get that foundation in. Easier said than done. With a stream in the way and foundation footings about three feet wide and a foot thick needed way below the streambed, our talents were truly tested. But we managed. We dragged in more fieldstone than most thought we'd ever use. Many cut stones were needed at corners and around window and door openings. Again these were found from barn foundations going to waste.

I was very lucky to find a set of 18th century casement windows from a dealer south of Montreal, complete with hardware. I had four of them

Armchair
Quebec, 1st quarter 18th century, Louis XIV maple and ash. An amazingly delicate chair for a giant to use.
H 48" W 26" D 21"

Armchair (below and opposite page)
Quebec, 1st quarter 18th century. Louis XIII and Louis XIV. Yellow birch and oak. It graced our home for a few days.
H 39" W 25" D 21"

arranged on the south wall for some useful passive solar heat that the stone floor generously gave back. With the deep windowsills you could sit with your legs out over the stream that washed the base of the building. Some period paneling in denim blue would become the room end with a Rumford-style fireplace centered in it. We had to thicken up the east gable wall to accept the depth of chimney. It all made for a cozy under-loft that contrasted dramatically with the high cathedral ceiling at the other end. Visitors often felt it to be chapel-like. The early, colorful Quebec furniture looked fantastic against them, and at home.

With furniture and supplies moved in, the edifice took on a life of its own. It seemed to have jumped through a wormhole in time, bringing with it a spiritual dimension that all who entered would respond to. Artist friends of all ages came from far and wide to draw and share their talent and ideas. It became a true atelier. Every Tuesday for years was set aside by all as community art day. The pond three steps from the door gave us trout by fly for lunch with swimming and general frolic among friends. I remember too, beautiful evenings when we'd shovel off the pond to skate under the big lantern above with smaller tin ones flickering around the edge. It was music. It was magic. It was a time forever etched in fond memories. I miss it to this day.

Small Box
Quebec, 18th century, deeply cut square panels, old red paint over original red, original staple hinges, replaced lock. The one that got away.
H 12.5" W 17.5" D 12"

Peace in the valley

with an 18th century gambrel reproduction overlooking a stream

When Shelley and I found that glorious twenty acres near Cavan we were at a loss to decide on the housesite. The land offered about everything you could ever wish for — high vistas over the valley or low down by the stream. There were a few promontories that could take a house quite well and fortunately, there was a great spot with fair access that could be cleared to take a few of the log houses I had in inventory. There were no neighbors to be seen, no matter where we settled. Of course I had to wind in a roadway to the house. That may have settled us on the lower ridge that overlooked the stream. It'd be too much work to take a road to the top and have to plough it every winter's day. Besides, being tucked under the hill, the house would avoid the north wind.

I suppose it was those visits to Old Deerfield that helped me decide on the style of the house. I was intrigued with the gambrels there and saw a few mechanical advantages they offered, not to mention the particular beauty of them that just looked so practical. It is always us against the elements isn't it? And the gambrel has proven itself for a long time.

The more we looked at the spot overlooking the stream, the more we liked it. I was beginning to see it. The east room would have French doors opening right out to the bush. Maybe sets of those "Indian shutters" for extra protection ... not for the New Englanders from Indians, but us from the weather. What better use of the knowledge gained during

those visits to Old Deerfield? When you meet so many antiquarians with a similar passion for old houses, you can't help but put it to use.

All of the forum guests were willing to share their knowledge. We would learn from each other while visiting the various 18th-century homes that lined the main street. And there were no out-of-bounds during the forums. We'd crawl into the dark corners of attics if we needed a closer look at roof construction. If we needed to measure or sketch some useful detail, we did. We would barrage the patrons, who we knew to be more knowledgeable than ourselves, with questions. They almost always offered satisfying and sometimes remarkable answers. We were of like mind in our quest to preserve our architectural history.

I knew there would be many details going into this gambrel that I learned at the forum. The copper flashing for instance. When I discovered that the wash from the rain on the copper flashing, particularly over the roof ridge, counteracted the mildew on cedar shingles, I knew to include that. And I liked those wooden rain gutters with a tin or copper liner. I did take a few pictures of it. The first time I went upstairs in one of the smaller gambrels, I fell in love with the style. It just felt so comfortable. I thought that space under the lower rafters would be a good place to hide the heat ducts, giving great access to all upper rooms.

I was able to get the address in Maine, for the supplier of their hand-riven clapboards. You certainly couldn't be more authentic than to use their product. And this next house of mine would put those wide pine boards I've saved to good use. I wanted wide floorboards and that horizontal wainscot for at least two of the rooms. And two boards for the chair rail. And now, for the doors, I could use those rimlocks I have, maybe even the Norfolk latches and the odd Suffolk — like the kind seen on the New England houses. I'd have to plan carefully for the wall colors. And I have to research the overall effect some more. It should look like those house interiors pictured in my White Pine Series.

It sure is going to be fun to furnish it. All those years of collecting the very early furniture will now pay off in beautiful rooms that look like they've been harboring a family for over a century. The trestle table would go in the library of course. The chair table's just right for the dining room. I'll use feather-edge sheathing on the fireplace wall, maybe in an old pewter color with the floors in yellow. They should go together well. And much of the fireplace hardware to go in the hearth and around the simple mantle.

Come to think of it, that could become a back-to-back fireplace, heating the dining room and the library. I'd probably put one of those Vermont Casting stoves, a small one, in the library. I think they're pretty practical, having those catalytic converters in them that allow for thirty hour burns. They come in a porcelain finish with quite a few colors too. All we need is the extra flue alongside the fireplace flue so it shouldn't cost much more. That wall would be three or four feet thick so perhaps I could take advantage of that by using the depth for the television and recording equipment. I don't see why not.

Open Hutch (preceding spread)
Ontario, c. 1830 Top 12" cut off with a chainsaw to fit in vendor's truck on the way to the Christie Antique Show. Expertly restored by Craig Black.

18th Century Mirror (above)
With original paint and decoration.

Gable (top)
The gambrel gable sheathed in shingles rather than clapboard, a cost saving in earlier times.

Six-Panel Door (bottom)
c. 1820 with transom, clapboards clinched with repro forged nails. Seth on guard for young thieves after two break-ins.

The Site (opposite page)
Set on the ridge overlooking the trout-filled stream. A young carpenter takes a break.

Twenty

years a slave

To a circa 1840 Stagecoach Inn and Tavern that needed decades of restoration

TWISS

Twiss Clock (opposite page)
Montreal, c. 1830, original mahogany paint graining. Always right twice a day.
H 83" W 12" D 9.25"

Pewter Cupboard
Dunnville Ontario, c. 1820, walnut, beaded doors, fluting detail, Germanic pieshelf, replaced brasses. Original blue paint stripped off by the vendor.
H 84.5" W 73" D 24"

"There's a house I think you'd better look at west of town." This from a realtor friend who knew the kind of place that might interest me. I'd been looking around Port Hope, Ontario, for about seven years for something worth restoring. When I saw the house, such as it was, set well back from the road with beautiful grounds surrounding it, four acres in all, I started to get excited.

"How did I miss this one?"

"Maybe you didn't," said my friend. "Put in an offer."

Well, even at a glance, I knew I would. The house had some great features, that of course had to be coaxed back into life and others that demanded an immediate demise, such as the "Tara" two-story porch that would come down with a good tug. It did. Only because I didn't ask for

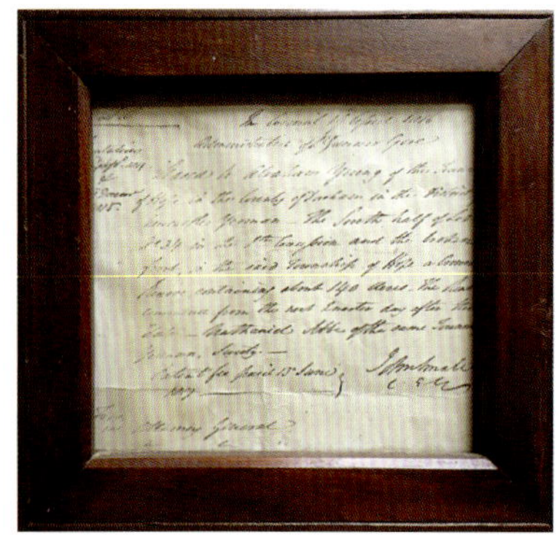

inclusions or offer less than the vendor asked for did I successfully outbid the four other offers presented that day. Sorry!

Compared to other houses in the area, this is a large house. It has a mid-century Georgian center hall, almost a full two stories high; actually what I would call a one-and-three-quarter, having a six-foot knee-wall which allowed for eight-over-eight panes that sat down close to the floor. There were only two original sashes left. Measuring the lower window jambs told me that twelve-over-twelves would be appropriate. Sometime later, my neighbor provided an early turn-of-the-century photo of a funeral party standing in front of the house and I was glad to see the entire sash intact. Supporting evidence can come from unexpected sources.

There was a kitchen addition that begged help and an attached woodshed that was just an eyesore. The interior had suffered one of those sixties "renovations" that it could have done without.

D.O

In Council 19th April 1816

Administration of Mr Governor Gore

Regulations of 4 Sept 1811 & 30 Decem 1815.

Leased to Abraham Young of the Township of Hope in the County of Durham in the District of Newcastle Yeoman – The South half of Lot No 34 in the 1st Concession and the broken front, in the said Township of Hope a Crown Reserve, containing about 140 Acres – The Rent to commence from the next Quarter day after this date – Nathaniel Abbe of the same Township Yeoman, Surety. –

Patent fee paid 13 June 1817

[illegible] C.E.C.

To The Attorney General

With four acres of grounds, I would now have lots of room to prebuild the period log homes in my inventory. It would involve, however, digging out about an acre of topsoil to the west side of the property and hauling in an equivalent amount of gravel for a good base. This, in itself, was quite an undertaking but another reason for this approach was business oriented.

It seems the house was known for many years as "Brandon Manor" and before that it was a tavern stop and inn, situated halfway between Newcastle and Port Hope. The public entered the centrally placed tavern door on the east gable end. A staircase from the tavern led to flophouse rooms on the second floor which explained the lack of doors into these rooms from the upper hall. The owners at that time lived privately on the west side of the house. The tavern room, being the largest in the house, would, of course, become the living room. When I happened across an original nine-foot-long bar with beautiful panels and a marble top, I had to find a place for it here. It was as if it had come home.

The front entrance was a scream, one of those Victorian remakes with colored glass. Zowie! It soon became obvious that the interior would have to be gutted. Start over. Save what we can of the original: three door frames, the floors, and three or four open-spring latches that are usually quite rare. But I had a few in inventory to replace the ones that were missing. And, of course, the great timber frame that was no worse for wear after 160 years of service. This was not a building where the timber frame was meant to show on the interior. That's another fad that has become a huge industry in itself in recent years. But originally, they were just structure.

There were remnants of panels below the parlor windows that inspired the style to be duplicated in the living room. The remaining door casings set the style for the new millwork. A cornice was added in the principal rooms as well as a boxed beam through the center of

Abstract (above)
My version of a new morning in an old frame.
H 13" W 17"+ frame

Deed (opposite page)
Property deed dated 1817 for 140 acres to Abraham Young.

Georgian Entrance (opposite page and top right)
Port Hope, 2001, installed into original frame opening, original door in original paint. Transom and sidelights with original, paneling and entablature reproduced by Charlie Schlegel.

Hurricane Lamp
New England, c. 1860.
H 14" D 9.5"

Dog (opposite page)
Blondie on the job guarding her daisies.

Chair
A reproduction of a Shaker desk chair in cherry and maple by master craftsman, Bruce Chambers.

Desk
c. 1820 from Burpee house in Sheffield N.B.
H 40" W 36" D 16"

the room containing wiring for the chandelier. There were some very nice period-style chandeliers available and I found a few at the Boston Restoration show. They work well if a dimmer switch is installed because ambiance is always a requirement. The slip room off the parlor became the drafting room. A modern pair of French doors was replaced with an early glazed door with transom above. This would lead to a large deck on the north side for those summer parties. Have to think ahead!

I could fill a book if I were to attempt to outline all of the various problems to overcome, procedures to establish (in order) and solutions required. Restoration can be a daunting task for anyone. Perhaps that's another story that calls for a room-by-room byplay, if one had the patience.

The true Shaker kitchen is spotless, ready for hungry workers at 5:30 a.m. — and doubtless the epitome of efficiency and craftsmanship among other things. Mine is not. Quite. Yet. It's true I took inspiration from the many aspects I have always admired about the Shaker ethic. I have always found their neat, unadorned spaces with their certain self-imposed restraint a principle to emulate. I had to respect their pared-down brevity of design that was nothing, if not practical. Utilitarianism was the chief principle employed in all their endeavors, whether architecture, furniture or farming. They put value on usefulness and efficiency, bringing a sincere honesty to every undertaking. We would not go too far wrong if we were to adopt some of the ideals the Shakers held dear to their hearts. I knew that if I could adhere to such a significant theme, I might gain a particularly rewarding abstract substance to the overall effect.

When it came time to add a kitchen at the end of my 1840 home, it seemed natural to pull together a few of those elements that might emulate the Shaker aesthetic while complementing my recently restored home.

I made a list of probable inclusions in the design; clean lines and surfaces, white walls with a plastered finish or facsimile thereof, and a period pine floor. A nice, naturally soft worn finish to the woodwork that's easy on the eyes and easy to live with (maybe a blue-gray). That chaste look they got with their cabinetry. Simple. Organized. Beautiful. And, of course, a large working fireplace, perhaps a wood ceiling and a few choice pieces of antique furniture. And how about a stone sink?

Small Cupboard (above, top left in image)
Waterloo, c. 1830, pine with blue paint over original, sat on kitchen chair rail, pie shelf. I sure regret selling this one.
H 20" W 20" D 8"

Table (above)
Alberta, c. 1820, Hutterite old red overpaint.
10' 9" x 2' 2"

There has to be lots of fenestration. The Shakers loved lots of light, as do I. Six-over-sixes should be the right scale. I'm beginning to get the picture. How about Dutch doors, one on each side of the room to get those nice summer breezes? It may seem like a long list but its not. It's less. And less is more. Right? They thought so. Me too. I may not go so far as to hang my chairs upside-down on the wall, but I may have a long sawbuck table with benches as they did.

I have an idea for the exterior that may work. Being by habit practical, the Shakers sometimes took the economical approach to siding a portion of their home. They shingled. No expensive clapboard needed. No paint. I like it. And it would complement the rest of the house that's covered in wooden ashlar. I think a granite chimney up the gable end would be nice

Woodbox (above)
Pine, c. 1840,
Quebec townships,
dovetailed case, original blue paint. About as much grace as you'd ever find in a woodbox.
H 48" W 32.5" D 21"

Apothecary (right)
New England, c. 1850,
eight drawers in original cream/green paint.
H 11" W 16" D 7"

as well. That puts the fireplace at the end of the room. Nice. Cozy. It was the fridge in the corner that set the order for the cabinet configuration. It seemed a strange idea at the time but it's worked out surprisingly well. Situated between the sink and the cooktop, that triangular plan that is so practical worked for me. And it maximized the available space. I thought of ways I might take advantage of those triangular corners on either side of the fridge. Since I like to bottle my own wine, I designed wine racks on one side and a small pantry on the other. Even a couple of cute drawers squeezed in.

I'm thinking like a Shaker now. I had originally planned for a six foot square island but when I found the ten foot sawbuck with benches it seemed a better choice since benches are among the most essential

Cupboards
Shaker-style with three layers of paint, corner fridge and wine pantry. How-to make a corner work.

Bowl
Native Abanaki burl bowl of Atlantic white cedar 18th century. Worn but well-loved.
19" x 11"

furnishings of the large Shaker dining areas. Believe it or not, the pair of benches and table came separately but had the same engine-red paint popular with the original Hutterite builders. I thought too, that the island would have sectioned the room somewhat. The table, however, integrated the service end and the fireside end while keeping the room open and engaging. And there have been many an occasion when that long table has served well. I could see two benches of Shakers enjoying a fine country-grown feast as guests at our dinner parties. It'd be quite a dance too, no doubt.

The piece-sur-

piece surprise

The perfect Quebec Habitant house for early Quebec antiques

Windows
In the casement style with 12 panes per side, single glazed with storms. A practical and tidy solution.

I'd just finished building one of our log homes near Cascades Quebec and found myself admiring the early buildings there, particularly the ones with the curved overhangs over their porches. Inevitably, I chose one to bring back to Ontario. It was large, being 35 feet by 28 feet with the customary *piece-sur-piece* method of extending wall length with upright posts.

The day after the truck arrived at our pre-building site we were sorting out the logs into four timbered walls when a snazzy car came into the driveway and a fellow got out to inspect our work. "What's that?" he asked. "It's a log house from Quebec," I answered. He just stood there with his mouth agape, almost in shock. A more appropriate client had yet to appear on our premises. When he found his voice he explained that he'd collected Quebec antiques for decades and had always wanted a Quebec house to keep them in. It seemed he knew enough not to step on serendipity's fickle foot and chose to follow her lead. He bought the building right then and there, as well as a couple of acres just north of Uxbridge in the following week. It turned out that Neil Darrach and I had some things in common, in particular our antiques, both of us loving the early Quebec pieces and both being watercolorists. During the course of the project we became friends and even went painting together. Of course the entire upstairs design was given over to his artistic pursuit.

The collecting bug bit Neil during his years as a business executive based in Montreal. It was while convalescing from a brief illness that he happened upon a copy of Jean Palardy's *The Early Furniture of French*

Canada, the same one I had at home. He was immediately enchanted with the styling of French Canadian furniture and Quebec antiques. His home showcased his collection of them soon afterwards. When he moved back to Ontario with his Quebec memorabilia, he kept adding to his collection with jaunts through rural areas surrounding Toronto. I suppose that brought him to our lane with the large hand-hewn letters "Tradition"carved into the massive log signage.

He immediately saw his future home there, laid out in rows of logs being numbered for reassembly. With little input from me, he envisioned the possibilities, probably even positioning his valued antiques on certain walls. Yes, he knew that a faithful reconstruction of a period Habitant home would perfectly suit the ancestry of his furniture collection. For Neil it was a natural and logical choice, offering the cosy warmth inherent in a log home as well as the special Quebec ambience he so admired. Although I knew little of the early days of the house, it was thought to have been home to a ship's captain in the 1820s. It was built on a riverside site near Rimouski, a town below Quebec City on the south side of the St. Lawrence. Architecturally, its French Canadian origins are obvious — the steeply pitched roof and the bellcast to the eaves are, of course, characteristic of old Quebec. Perhaps less typical is the log construction, which although not unknown in the province, was generally reserved for temporary shanty dwellings until a more substantial stone building could be erected.

But back in the here and now, Neil and I put our thoughts together, applying our combined knowledge to his requirements for comfortable retirement living. Many period elements were incorporated into the plan, including early casement windows as well as a charming stairway from the 1780s that I happened to have in inventory. It even had its original

Fireplace
In the 18th century style as designed by Count Rumford, once an apprentice country storekeeper in Salem, Massachusetts, named Benjamin Thompson.
H 42" W 44" D 20"

Chair
Shepherd's wing chair, 19th century with original paint.
H 48" W 29"

Armoire
Quebec, early 19th century, doors with lozenge panels, remains of original green paint.
H 76" W 43" D 16"

red paint. A handsome glazed cupboard, also painted in rustic hues, was built into the dining room wall to lend an air of tradition. Despite these touches of antiquity, the house boasted all the amenities desirable for contemporary living. Space was set aside for ample walk-in closets, two baths and adequate storage. A special nook was reserved for Neil to use as a studio where he produces watercolors up to five hours a day. The highlight of this house is the warmth of its log construction, which represents a cozy sense of "home" conducive to relaxation. Today, friends and family often remark how comfortable they feel as they sit by the fire, surrounded by the charm of the natural wood. Comments inevitably turn to furniture — the diamond point and other pieces that lend the collection its authentic French Canadian flavor. For a moment, a visitor might imagine they are actually in a home in the Quebec countryside, and for Neil, perhaps that's the kindest compliment of all.

Drive Shed/Garage
Quebec, c. 1800, reconstructed for modern use. Original blue door and suffolk latch (above). Somehow, incredibly lifted onto a new foundation.

Table
Quebec, early 19th century, pine and hardwood, found in convents, eight drawers. A drawer per nun? H 30" W 120" D 36"

Bellcast Roof
Curved plywood extensions applied to existing rafters to carry overhang without posts.

Beams (opposite page)
Quebec, c. 1800, hand-hewn ceiling beams with extra bracing by the ship owner.

The Great

Pretender

"Who'd have thought our house would fool the historians? From then on the house has always been deemed 'The Great Pretender,'" said Helen.

Fifty years in the restoration or reproduction of period houses often offers unexpected challenges. Dr. Morley for instance, was particular about having a period style house, so particular that we drove over most of southern Ontario picking out what we agreed were the nicest, pertinent features of mid-century stone houses — leaving out the bric-a-brac and fancy stuff that often pushed its way into loose interpretations of the style.

The plan evolved until we were all on the same blueprint page. But when they showed me the steep hillside available on their newly acquired lot, I must admit, I had misgivings. We knew a walk-out to the back to access the forest would have to be part of the plan.

Obviously, some serious tiering of the slope was needed. Three major levels were required. Fortunately, we had a good excavator who knew how to tear up the land just right (and put it back just right too, after the house was built).

A larger challenge now faced us — the stones. On our fact-finding missions we often found ourselves aghast at the size of the stones those masons threw around in the old days. Enormous didn't quite cover it. But we had to have them, didn't we? I thought back to the fireplace we built on my first log house in1967 near Uxbridge. I remembered that we'd salvaged those stones that climbed up the logs from a few local barn foundations, particularly those monstrous corner stones. Maybe there were enough old barn foundations still to be found… and scrounged?

Mantle
Ontario, c. 1830, neoclassical firebox entablature.
H 48" W 50"

Balusters (opposite page)
A simple design, tapered at each end that wasn't simple to lathe-turn at all.

Well, there were. Six or seven, in fact. That's a lot of really old (we like old) hand-crafted Precambrian granite corners to be reused.

Truckload after truckload deposited them around our foundation. Acres of them. No one seemed to believe me when I kept saying, "keep 'em coming." You soon couldn't see the forest for the stones. Finally, I said, "Stop!" Would you believe, that after months of the really hard labor of lifting the monsters one-by-one into place, we were only short about six stones. Especially the big one that master mason Glen Ward carved the name "Morley" onto then set proudly near the top of the north gable.

There were other challenges too, perhaps not so daunting … like how to reproduce those folding interior shutters to fit perfectly … and in choice mahogany, no less. Or how to accommodate an "old English style" water-collecting cistern into the basement… while not having the rainwater collectors show on the exterior. Or how to produce a simple stair spindle with just the right taper at its top and bottom (each different of course).

Oh well, all easy stuff, after the fact. Helen and Tom Morley took twenty years to consider the possibilities for a new house on their fifty-acre property just north of Toronto. There were other priorities in those early days: raising a family, managing a home in the city, not to mention his-and-hers medical careers. In the meantime however, the land was well-taken care of. They had family picnics regularly, and planted spruce and pine trees to stabilize the slopes.

A time came to start a plan. Gradually a picture developed of the Morley's favorite features to be included in the design of their new house-to-be. The Morleys were determined to build something that fit into the landscape.

"And nothing fits into the Ontario countryside better than an old Ontario farmhouse, especially one built of stone," Tom says. "So that's what we built. The irony is, however, that the house looks as old as the hills. Although new from the ground up, it could easily pass for an 1850 farmhouse. With its granite-stone construction and handsome gables, it bears a striking resemblance to local century homes.

"It looks like it's been there all along," Tom remarks. "That was our goal." Conventional or not, the house was rendered so convincingly that it appeared mistakenly in a recent inventory of local heritage structures. "How soon they forget," quips Tom. "Who'd have thought our house would fool the historians?" From then on the house was always deemed "The Great Pretender."

Datestone
Ontario's pretty-old, Precambrian granite for a 1980 datestone carved and lifted into place by Glen Ward and a strong helper.

It was important to site the house to take advantage of the views with large and generous windows, as well as the veranda and balcony. Using the existing topography to advantage, the house was built on the hillside, the one with a panoramic vista from every room. It was the site too, with enough slope that the basement would walk out at ground level at the rear.

Of course we built in many features to have the house feel more authentic: a fine set of period doors, a reclaimed neo-classical fireplace mantel, old-style window sash with small panes, and cedar shingles for the roof. Our cabinetmaker planed proper moldings on baseboards. Even interior window shutters were made (a first for us), especially for Tom's office, in custom walnut. Our master mason used vintage stone-laying techniques. Though called a veneer, the stones were up to ten inches thick and accounted for a lot of sweat on the job.

Less than an hour from the skyscrapers of the city, the Morleys, with our help, had created the perfect home environment. A new old house. A restored landscape. Who could ask for anything more?

Well, there was one more thing. Tom and I became great friends, often sharing the same canoe as we explored Ontario's most challenging

rivers. So that's the story about the Morley house. But some stories carry on as they should, much as we do, into lives yet unknown and adventures in themselves.

The new owners named Willson became the custodians of the home they'd have chosen for themselves, even acknowledging the Morley name of the house by leaving the name forever engraved and intact in the chimney stone.

With a willing and earnest responsibility Grant and Jane will restore where necessary those aspects that require their help, while no doubt putting their own stamp and character to the task to make it their own as well.

The fact that the full basement housed little else but a water cistern (something that Tom Morley thought was a good idea), was now unneeded. The space however, presented a great opportunity for an entertainment area for the family and an art studio for Jane. They were able to find artisans to create a wonderful plan for the space. Having found an early 19th century billiard table locally, it would become the centerpiece of the Arts-and-Crafts-style family room. Other period pieces in the style surround the table.

Then came the task to take better advantage of the potential vistas from the summit of the hill. They engaged me to design the fenestration

that would open up the kitchen to the west view that looks out over fifty acres of forest and great sunsets. I found a way to do it with large eighteen-pane windows on either side of a pair of French doors that covered the entire width of the room. The French doors of course, would open to the balcony, which was large enough for breakfast or lunches on beautiful days. The idea was realized, letting nature right into the house.

Jane had some ideas for her studio, with its wide pine wallboards and floors that would shine their golden glow to let a little more light in. Glen Ward, our master mason for many years — yes, he who put up (with help) those huge granite blocks of stone wherein the Willsons now reside — came out of retirement to help. He added the new matching window provided in the south wall that looks as though it had always been there.

Extensive landscaping was required also, to account for the severe slopes of the three-tiered hillsite. Now one could drive around the two-car garage right up to the north balcony steps. Even some underground storage was cleverly built into the hill. Some very dramatic house-scapes were seen when approaching the house on the hiking trails to the west.

It seems The Morley House has fallen into the right hands.

So that's the story about the Morley house. But some stories carry on as they should, much as we do, into lives unknown and adventures in themselves. New owners have chosen to be the custodians that would carry the legacy on. The Willsons have picked up the gauntlet, or should we say, the hammer and saw and all the other tools needed to take the house into the next century in good order, perhaps at some point passing it on to the next generations who may appreciate it. It's not unlike passing the baton in the race that requires responsibility and a certain commitment, not to mention the honoring of the former owners.

There was even a walkout to the lower garden. Glen Ward even came back to add a south window in the stone wall for Jane. It looked like it had always been there. It seems the Morley house has fallen into the right hands.

Staircase
Uxbridge, Ontario, c. 1840, recycled, in original finish, to gain entrance to the restored lower level. We never say "basement."

Billiard Table (right and opposite page top and bottom)
c. 1940, found in Port Hope, Ontario, various hardwood veneer in original finish. No deep pockets allowed.

THE CURRENT OWNERS COMMENT:

"Once in a while a little magic enters ones lives. For Grant and I it occurred in 2007 while we were mountain biking on Concession 6, just north of Claremont.

It was a glorious April morning. We had just exited a trail in the Durham Forest and found ourselves on one of the most picturesque roads you can imagine. As we looked to our right we spotted a sale sign on the property of a magnificent stone house. The house was perched on a hill radiant with daffodils, like a scene straight out of a famous William Wordsworth poem. How unusual this seemed to us. Typically a 19th century stone Manor would have been located front row center on a sprawling farm property. Yet this house was situated on a hill facing towards acres of forest! Our curiosity was piqued and we rode our bikes up to the backdoor and knocked.

Two charming octogenarians, Tom and Helen Morley, answered the door and invited us in for tea. During the conversation that followed, they explained that they had conceived of the house from a dream of their English past. They had completed the house in 1981 and referred to it as 'The Great Pretender,' explaining that this was a new house possessing modern amenities yet had all the classic elements of a Georgian manor. As we sipped our tea, Helen looked me directly in the eye. She

BAILEYS

held my gaze and pointed her finger as if casting a spell. 'You're going to buy this house!' she proclaimed. And of course we did!

Since purchasing 'The Morley House' we have carried on the dream of this house being 'The Great Pretender.' To this end the Morley's directed us to Mel Shakespeare who agreed to helped us where needed as we determined that the house was not quite finished.

Outside of the house we embarked on extensive landscaping. We were lucky to get in touch with Glen Ward, the original mason who had worked on the house from 1979 to its completion. Fortunately he agreed to take up the challenge and share his invaluable masonry skills. Glen managed to create stunning gardens, pathways and retaining walls that nestled the house beautifully into the terraced hills. The house seems finished now. What the Morleys began, we have completed with careful attention to the 'heritage' of this absolute gem of a house.

Grant and I will always remember that sunny day in April — the day that we met Tom and Helen Morley, and Helen chose to cast her spell on us! The magic lives on."

— Grant and Jane Willson

The Bar (opposite page)
The Willson's hired a cabinetmaker to construct a rustic bar to complement their new family room. There must be a lot of bar tabs in all of those drawers.

Art Sudio
Wide pine floors, new south window, French doors, tin ceiling.

Garage
I don't know why we didn't design a window into the front.

41

The coop de ville

The chickens were evicted. They were feeling cooped up anyway.

Mrs. Harrop is now the ruler of the roost.

I'd traveled that old road hundreds of times and never paid much attention to a board and batten chicken coop that rested sad and forgotten along the highway. But on this particular day curiosity got the better of me and I found myself driving up to the farmer's house. When he came out, I asked if I could have a look at the old building.

That's when he gave me the story of his angry encounter with another guy that came to him with the same question. But he did let me take a quick look inside. I must say I was more than pleasantly surprised. Though small, it was a post and beam one-and-a-half story house with lovely hand-hewn floor joists that carried the second floor. This may have become a chicken coop but they were sure living in style. They had the remains of a classic 1840 fireplace with paneled wainscoting around the living room, topped off with a nice chair-rail molding. Even the original wide pine floors had survived. Sure, they'd been painted with a thick splattering of you-know-what, but that is easily removed with a careful spray wash. I could even detect the original paint underneath. It seemed I'd stumbled on a gem.

Stenciled Walls
In the 19th century manner by Jewel Harrop and Sandra Spearing.

Addition (above and opposite page, top)
The lean-to becomes a charming tearoom for guests.

Mural (opposite page, bottom)
Also by Jewel and Sandra, showing Jewel's previous home of the 19th century where most of her antiques had resided.

Then the farmer began his story. "The guy seemed to want it badly but he only offered me a thousand for it. I was really insulted," he said.

So of course I asked him what he wanted.

He came back with, "Make me an offer."

Without giving it too much thought, I told him, "I'll give you twice that." It seemed to be what he wanted to hear, so, as quick as you could cluck, "Cock-a-doodle-doo!" I suddenly had a deluxe chicken coop soon to fly into inventory. Of course I didn't market it as that.

Shortly, perhaps in the same week after that incident, I got a call from a woman who I later learned was the twin sister of an elderly lady named Jewel Harrop. Evidently, her very sick sister was asking for me, although I'd never heard of her at this point. I asked the sister what it was about but she refused to answer the question, just that it was important I meet her as she requested.

Well, I was given the name of the hospital in Lindsay. I found my way to her room to find Mrs. Harrop in a seemingly comatose state. I was

about to leave when she asked, "Is that you, Mel? Oh, thanks for coming. I'm sorry you see me this way but I haven't been myself lately since my husband died. I don't know what to do. My sister says my idea is crazy. You know, not having a home anymore is depressing me. I've collected all those articles about your houses for years and knew you might have something, just small of course. My name is Jewel by the way."

So that's what this is about, I thought. I immediately recalled the chicken coop that wasn't a chicken coop. I even had pictures on my iPhone of it before and after takedown. I cued them up and handed Jewel the phone. As she looked at the pictures her pallor brightened and her eyes grew big and eager. She was transforming right then and there, morphing in front of me like a shape-shifter. It looked like she was about to jump out of bed and run out to buy a hardhat and hammer.

I was surprised that she knew what she was looking at. This led to a long discussion of her own period home full of wonderful antiques that were now in storage, and her adventures through some of the same historic villages that I loved too. We were obviously of like mind.

It was also the first time I conducted a design meeting on a hospital bed. She had the nurses all out hunting paper and pencils for me so her ideas could be taken down and roughly positioned somewhere in the coop... oops, house. We eventually had to borrow a table from a doctor's office. Jewel somehow convinced two male nurses to maneuver it into her cramped room. And the hospital food she ordered up wasn't really as bad as the common gossip contents.

There came a time when I had enough information to be able to develop this further. I urged her to get well and call me when she felt up to another design session, hopefully, somewhere else. From the new anticipation I saw in her eyes, I expected to hear from Jewel soon. There weren't many clients who could visualize it right away. She was one.

As it turned out, she bought the coop, found a nice lot in the middle of Lindsay and in a short time was herself installed in her small dream house. The house had become her hobby and decorating it her outlet for self-expression. I was surprised at her expertise regarding the old colors and their application, using them imaginatively to play off each other, never afraid to use strong colors like they did in the past. Jewel agreed with me and would never use drywall.

One of the trickiest challenges was deciding how and where to build in a kitchen. We sectioned a portion off of the dining room to the south. It was to be six or seven feet deep and it was to look like a deep open hutch, wall-to-wall. She saw it immediately in a faded gray-blue — before being built, of course. Her artistic self always took command.

"Rough plaster for the walls looks more rustic," she'd say. "And in an early house like this bold tones make all the difference." There were times when life under construction proved more than a little frustrating, partly because she had to move in before the house was ready.

"The rewards were worth the wait," she said. "And then, I was on hand every day to supervise the work, but I didn't want to rush it either. Why hurry?" She paid particular attention to the colors and stenciling in the dining room, the biggest room in the house. Her good friend Sandra Spearing, a decorative painter, helped considerably. Their collaborative effort created a Rufus Porter-style wall mural, something you don't see in a resurrected chicken coop every day. They began by rendering the wall in a flat oil paint and wash. Then the fun really started with folky freehand sketches of rural farmscapes. Part of it even depicted Jewel's previous home.

Jewel was a woman with few doubts and her intentions were carried out quite well. On many occasions we talked about the countless museum villages we'd been to in New England, often the same ones. She'd become quite an antiquarian in her own right. It was a pleasant experience for both of us, in part because with her antiquarian's eye she knew what she wanted, even down to the period fencing around the lot. She had us back a few years later to add a sunroom to the south. I'd been back a few times for tea over the years to chat about antiques and old houses.

Gate (**opposite page**)
Historical picket fence design from 19th century with the ingenious ball and chain weight that self-closes the gate.

Lantern (**opposite page**)
Even Jewel's outdoor lighting is to period, right down to the chamfered post.

41

A journey back

to the past

A bold move for an Ontario classic from Bolton to Queensborough

Upper Hall
An exceptionally wide upper hall, for a house of this vintage. If you don't have a ball court or a putting green, roll up the rug for long ones or just move in some large furniture.

Southern Ontario is a treasure trove of early architecture for those inclined to history. And it is the abundance of its various histories represented in visual architectural form that adds to its interest and beauty. In my expeditions through the countryside and towns, I always spare an eye for the homes of our past. Often these are in need of salvage or preservation, though vestiges of their former prestige may be glimpsed if one were to look carefully. Going through Bolton one day many years ago, I stopped to inspect a brick house in the process of demolition. What caught my eye was not so much the definitive Italianate aspect of it dominating the scene, but an earlier house that peeked out from under the brick veneer. Seldom had I seen such a graphic example that shows how existing architecture is manipulated to showcase the perceived refinement that happens to be popular at the moment, the moment in this case being about 1890 or so.

There, behind the bricks that were being stripped off, in seemingly great condition, was a clapboard house of great proportion that I suspected was a mid-19th century timber frame that had been hidden for about half a century. I had to check this out. Yes, it was intended for demolition — destruction actually, except for the brick that the salvage yard had purchased. I very soon determined the underlying construction. It had excellent bones — hand-hewn timbers in fact, that I knew dated it to perhaps 40 to 50 years before the disguise it now wore. It was a house of straightforward honest expression with little use of intricacy and unwarranted expression; deep window jambs that housed the posts, beautiful wide pine flooring, a paneled wainscoting and other lovely features deserving a better fate than this. The central hall plan with its generous front entrance sported sidelights and transom still intact. A particularly spacious upper hall was a surprise that would allow for furniture not normally found in such a space. I would have liked to have thanked that someone who very carefully "bricked it" so that the original structure was left pretty much unharmed. No, the garbage dump was not going to swallow this one!

My offer was accepted and I sent a crew to dismantle it with care. Surely, someone would appreciate this one. Not that the house with its brick veneer was unappreciated. It was a most handsome representative of an era that followed the more simple, quiet aesthetic of Ontario's early settlers. The early house became old and change was due. A house that served for many decades had new owners; a product of its time, circumstance and personal taste. Why not resurface the building? Dressing up, veneering and recycling were part of a progressive society that insisted on moving forward. A brick house was considered "first class." The more modest beginnings were disapproved of and too often lost to memory and decay. It was not uncommon for the new, popular gothic details to be superimposed over the more chaste lines that had lasted for more than a century, if not centuries. In this vanguard of change it would not be remiss to consider some attempts to be pretentious. Every man's home is his castle, or at least, his interpretation of one. It's all "in the eye of the beholder," as they say.

We began the process of careful salvage. Every piece of woodwork was numbered and documented — even the clapboards, though it turned out they would not appear again on the reconstruction. They were worn a little too thin, the natural consequence of age. We were most happy to find that the post-and-beam frame itself was as sound as the day it was

Cupboards (opposite page)
Cabinetry for library/living room by Grant Eskerod.

Seasonal
A house for all seasons, particularly when set in a fifty-acre winter wonderland.

built. And, shortly after we had it carefully stored away, I was to meet the Chants, Don and Merle, who would become the new custodians of this house, the former Taylor house, one of the oldest houses in Bolton. Thus, a legacy is passed from the homeowner in one century to the homeowner in another.

I think the craftsmen who first built the place would be happy to know that it still lives and is lovingly cared for today.

Arbor
Through rare shrubs and trees, take the walking trails over the 50 acres or just sit on the porch for tea afterwards. Garden trellis and bellcast porch by Grant Eskerod.

THE CURRENT OWNERS PASS ON THESE THOUGHTS:

"We have been city-dwellers most of our lives (the sixties through the eighties), in Toronto. In the late eighties, with retirement peeking over the horizon, we decided to leave the city for all the usual reasons: congestion, smog, noise, lack of privacy, and so on. That meant finding a place in the country. We both like old houses with a sense of history and past lives lived. We had spent many happy summers in Prince Edward County so that is where we began our search. At first we looked for an old house on an interesting property. After a year of fruitless searching, we abandoned this approach. At about that time we came into contact with Mel Shakespeare and learned that he had a circa 1837 timber-framed house stored in a barn west of Toronto, each piece numbered and ready for reassembly. From that point on we limited our search to an area where this house could be moved. Again, we had no luck in Prince Edward County, so we switched our focus to Hastings County, north of there. Eventually we found the perfect place — 50 acres with wooded hills, and a small creek. It was about six miles north of the town of Madoc, near the hamlet of Queensborough, once thriving during a mini gold rush.

We chose a site well-removed from the road and here the reconstruction began in late 1991. The process of reconstruction was interesting, to say the least, much like putting together a Lego set, with care taken to insure that each numbered piece fitted into its proper place. The basic house was in remarkably good shape after 164 years of life, though some parts were simply too old to be used again, for example the original clapboards. Nevertheless, the house was ready for occupancy in the spring of 1992 and was transformed into a home. We have lived in it happily for many years and feel totally committed there. When we moved in, the land surrounding the house was a barren building site but over the years we have changed that with extensive, mostly native tree and shrub planning and the nurturing of gardens.

We value the land as much as the house, with its varied topography and vegetation, and many species of wildlife, from bears, foxes and coyotes, to raccoons, muskrats, and beavers. In order to protect this environment in perpetuity we entered into a covenant with the Nature Conservancy of Canada, which does not permit any disturbance of the land. One thing we learned from this adventure is that no matter how we cherish the old house, the need for maintenance and plain old fixing up is endless and unrelenting. It has helped us learn more about the house and to bond with it even more closely. Each year that passes we feel that not only has our home become part of us, but also we have become a part of it, writing the next chapter for a building that has lived through so many decades and experienced so many other lives about which we know so little."

— Don And Merle Chant at Lark Rise

Two centuries later

A house from Stoney Creek, with an historic Canadian history, lives again

I'm not sure now how I found myself in Stoney Creek that day. Perhaps I was following a lead to some old house or other. I knew it was an early Ontario settlement area. I couldn't help but notice what appeared to be an abandoned house, sitting forlorn and neglected not far off the road. It was a big one for sure. I reckoned about fifty feet wide at least. That had my curiosity up. There was something about it that demanded my attention. The first thing I noticed was the wide spacing between the upper three windows. It sure looked to me like there were two more hidden under the stucco façade.

Then too, of course, there were those Victorian elements that looked out of place, what I considered to be clues of evidence; those soffit brackets, the bay windows, even an iron railing bracket cresting the roof peak. I imagined the clapboard siding that's hopefully under the stucco. Then, of course, we'd find a huge post and beam frame, the hand-hewn skeleton, usually of the local pine. That would be typical of such massive homes like this one, that I was looking at — entranced.

I pictured in my mind the correct placement of twelve-over-twelve windows, five in all, that would bring a more correct proportion to light. I was sure the interior studs would offer the verification. Given the opportunity and a bit of luck, a large story may have been unfolding. There could have been a real treasure here, ready to cast off some old clothes, to display even older ones, the kind I love to see. I knew I wasn't going to let this one get away, not if I could help it and if it hadn't been sold or spoken for already.

It didn't take too long to find and deal with its owner. Tradition Home Designs Inc. now had an historic jewel in inventory. Subsequent exploration proved my assumptions right. It turned out to be a magnificent example of a Georgian home from the early years of the 19th century, 1817 in fact. And what a history it had. I later found that it related back to Laura Secord herself, the heroine of the War of 1812. Historical record proved the builder to be Elijah Secord, Laura Secord's nephew.

Most Canadians know her story. Courageously, Laura, a staunch Loyalist, had hiked about twenty miles from the occupied American territory in 1813 (just four years before the house was built) to warn the British forces of an impending American attack. With similar character,

she rescued her husband, James Secord, who was wounded at the Battle of Queenston Heights. She dutifully nursed him to recuperation at home. I am always heartened to find such histories attached to houses, especially those of this vintage. I expect it will always stay with the house, no matter who becomes its guardian. No stones went unturned in order to establish the facts that could lead us to the most accurate restoration. Evidently, an elderly Secord descendant remembered the house and offered a few interior details that were helpful.

Before I would be taking it down, I usually put out the word to a few potential clients who just may love it. At this time, I had just finished a large period log home on Airport Road, near Stirling Ontario, for Conrad and Lois Kuebler. They had mentioned the house that I was offering to their good friends, Bob and Ginny Palliser, who had built a reproduction in early style to contain their growing antique collection. It seems they had been thinking they might need a bigger house for their growing family as well.

The Pallisers had grown up in Belleville and were living near the small town of Stirling when Bob spotted my ad for the Stoney Creek house in *Century Home* magazine. He may also have seen a few of their articles that had featured our homes after they had been built and moved into, usually featuring the owners antique collections. The couple had long shared a passion for historic buildings and antiques. With their two sons they were living in a recently-built dwelling that was designed to look old, a house that lacked the character of a period dwelling. They realized that the Stoney Creek structure would allow them to retreat to a more rural country setting that was secluded and live in a home with the authenticity they were looking for.

So they were among the first to come and see it for themselves. When I pointed out the wonderful features still intact in the house, they started to get excited about it. I only had to offer a few ideas that could certainly bring it back to life before they saw the potential of the project. I think they saw it with their antiques carefully arranged in the many rooms available.

When we got further into the architectural plans, which developed naturally from the evidence at hand, we had documented seven working Rumford fireplace hearths. All were eventually restored with early mantelpieces. We didn't have to create the center hall plan. It was what it was, including the later newel post and stair rails from the Victorian

Door (above)
In the early 18th century manner with bullseye transom, HL hinges and period latches.

Garage
Keeping to the age, the saltbox style seems appropriate. Notice the close-to-the-weather clapboards, with hand-forged nails.

era. It was expertly done and would stay in the house as part of its history to date.

I had a nice collection of early door hardware that was employed to add authenticity. It was the wonderful floors that were salvaged, laying atop the hand-hewn beams, that gave most of the interior charm to the whole. They cleaned up nicely, glowing with that wonderful patina that only age provides. The wide board wooden walls had to be sawn and edged in the old way, some beaded, others feather-edged, to complete the principal rooms — not to mention, giving them the old colors they may have worn one-hundred-and-seventy-years ago.

John Riddle was just the man to prepare the wall boards. He was an excellent cabinetmaker and had been working on our jobs for a few years. I figured he'd still have those knives that cut the feather-edges for

Secret (above)
Removal of the top of the newel post reveals a hidey-hole for the owner's private property deed. Oh, oh, now it's not a secret. Sorry.

Aerial
A view of the property amid the forest from the air.

the wainscot or walls. Anything that just needed beading would also be a snap. The exterior basically took its original shape with no real argument other than removing some later unneeded carpentry or embellishment.

Sometimes the breaks in the floorboards would reveal the size of the fireplace — the kitchen fireplace often showing us where the bake oven would have been. This was the case here, so consequently, that would be an important restoration for the mason. I'm not sure if the bake oven was ever used. Another back-to-back pair of fireplaces offered another benefit: creating a passage between the rooms. Another passageway hid a pantry, refrigerators, freezers and wall ovens, an altogether handy arrangement. The kitchen cabinets with their soapstone countertop wonderfully complimented the room.

I am always afraid that when a house is turned over to its new custodians, anything may happen, often to the detriment of the love, care and fastidiousness of the owners who tried to do justice to the house, having given their best effort to produce such an accurate example of the early period of our shared history. Thus, anyone who follows in their footsteps may study and enjoy.

Oven (opposite page)
Stoney Creek, Ontario, 1817 bake oven and fireplace hearth reconstructed near Stirling Ontario in late 1990s.

Lock (above)
A period rimlock, c. 1840, English with exceptional brass embellishment.

Cupboard
Quebec, c. 1840, with original salmon and green/gray paint, missing drawer.
H 60" W 43" D 16"

In good hands

VALLEYVIEW FARM

A restoration
...three times
a charm

The first time I saw Valleyview Farm was the chance to buy it... actually, trade ours for this available stone house. Jean and I had purchased an eight acre property just west of Uxbridge and we were into vast plans to enlarge it. The stone house did have potential but it was not in the best shape. Maybe the large hole in the living room floor was what put us off. You could have driven a small car into it.

I supposed the objective was to let the heat up from the furnace in the basement. So after careful consideration, we did not do the swap. I did however, a few years later, get the job to restore the house. There was certainly lots to do.

Fortunately, my second set of clients, John and Adele Sebert, were up to the task and brought much creativity of their own to the job. They helped to make good choices when offered options. It was time to save, change or discard. Their collection of vintage memorabilia found wall space throughout the house, adding colors it hadn't seen in its 120 year history. There were whirligigs, trade signs of every description, tobacco tins, saxophones, folk art, toy cars, each and all graphic and complimentary of each other. John and Adele's combined history working in the film and advertisement field gave flair in all aspects of the restoration.

We kept the original colors when possible, avoiding the stripping of paint. Adele chose the wonderful red for the new kitchen, having learned many tricks from the set decorators she had worked with. Her extensive and rare collection of spongeware pottery that she started in the early 60s added her own touch to the scene as well.

Two workable fireplaces were needed and Glen Ward, our master mason went to work. I found a nice period mantle and a gray-blue color for it as well as the room's deep window wells with their canted panels. All rooms came alive, offering a welcome, comfortable ambiance throughout. John also had Glen build a stone garage for his exotic European racing cars. It started with his collecting car advertising as a child and he'd been tinkering with cars ever since, not that you could really call it tinkering — he was actually racing them, entering eight to ten races every year. The Seberts led energetic lives, ranging from fast cars, fine wines, antiques and great food, living life with spirit and adventure. When they eventually moved into Port Hope I was happy to help them with that house too.

House
A handsome stone farmhouse built in 1847 in Neo-classic tradition near Port Perry, Ontario, beautiful fanlight and sidelights, restored throughout for three separate clients over many years.

Racing Car
John with his 1936 Frazer-Nash racing car originally owned by Lord Beaverbrook's son.

Kitchen
Adele chose a red for her new kitchen with comfortable hearth and a fridge hidden behind the door.

Fireplace
A new firebox and fireplace mantle, c. 1840, in gray/blue.

Window
Canted and paneled window wells with weather vane/whirligig.

It was a few years after that when I got the call again. Valleyview Farm had new owners. David Leroy and John Peever called me for some design work, needing ideas for a room between the stone house and the garage. They were hoping something interesting could be done with the space. I could see from their furnishings and the care they'd exercised for the place that the house had come into good hands, always a good position to start out in. It wouldn't be a huge room but it could be quite comfortable. Many clients think big rooms are ideal when, in fact, they can be uncomfortable to live in.

I set about to determine the feasibility of the wall and roof structure, finding it substantially out of square and out of plumb. This had to be rectified if decent fitting of new material was to be possible, especially

Windows
A gang of four to light the room to the west with a view to the pool and garden.

considering the new windows and entrance had to fit properly. So the end walls were totally rebuilt. When they told me they wanted the room to look very early they were lucky on two counts. First, I had the material; early flooring, hand-hewn beams for the ceiling, and the wide, beaded wallboards, all of it probably earlier than their 1847 home. Secondly, at the moment, two expert craftsmen were available to do the work required. They were a fifty-year-old pair of Germanic twins that were skilled in most of the building trades but particularly skilled for what we had in mind. When outlining a job to them (with a clear set of designs, of course) it was like speaking to one mind. And you didn't have to repeat yourself. They both understood immediately. I was used to seeing jobs well done but the twins seemed to go beyond the expected. Fitting those beams together seamlessly as they did, impressed everyone. David was on the same page when it came to maintaining the finish on those very rare beams. He first washed them ever so carefully then, once dry, he used a drill with a soft nylon brush to take them from a gray hue to bring up their more natural color. He also installed the flooring, a puzzle he solved, with every board being a different width. Fortunately, most were the width of the room, which helped.

The wallboards all had some color but in the end David stripped them down to a soft pine. We weren't sure if we had enough to do the job until we neared the end. Yes, only a few scraps left. When my plans for the windows and doors were approved they set about to make the walls to accommodate them. One particularly interesting aspect of the job was

Television
The ship's panel over the fireplace latches up to the ceiling beam to reveal the large TV. A cute idea eh?

The Room
An early 19th century reproduction for a linking room between the stone house and the garage, period beamed ceiling, period floors, and wide period beaded wallboards. The Polex Twins, Gerd and Bernd, did a masterful job.

the creation of the secret door. I've always loved secret doors in a house. My library in the Cavan house had one. An entire section of books (that must have weighed a ton) swung out effortlessly with a fingertip. It was to pass into an eventual addition which, unfortunately, never happened. This one was to pass from "The Room" to the garage. The key was to see nothing that suggested there was a door there at all, just a board wall. Of course it took interesting hinge hardware to make it work, given the accuracy required.

The wall offered another opportunity as well. David's idea of using the space given by the wall depth for the television worked wonderfully. Centered over the fireplace, the panels were pulled up and hooked to the ceiling beam, simplicity itself. The width of the room helped account for the comfort as the leather couch sat opposite of course.

And what a beautiful contrast — that leather against those wonderfully majestic stones. And the light tucked under the beam was a nice touch too. I expect the Labradors liked their new room. After all, didn't

they start the idea? A few extra scratches on those old floorboards would hardly be noticed.

The new Georgian entrance with its sidelights sure added some grace and light to the whole thing. David found the perfect rimlock for the glazed door. And the entrance looked pretty good in white against the blue exterior boards. I sure was impressed when I went back for pictures once it was furnished. The room had become one of the great features of the house, often difficult when the house was already pretty great.

It can only happen when the house is in good hands.

The Foyer
A quasi-checkerboard-marbleized entrance hall standing out graphically, dividing the living room and music room.

Kitchen Wall (opposite page)
The use of simple wall paneling in off-white, with storage under the back stairs.

Garage
A granite stone garage sports a tall classical window on the board and batten gable ends.

Quilt
An eye-catching quilt lays casually as can be on the backstairs railing that sports a wonderful blue paint.

Portrait (opposite page)
A pair of spaniels guard an as-found portrait, including the gilt frame, grace an upstairs bedroom.

What lies beneath?

Could we be so lucky?

Our early history suggests the reasonable assumption that log homes were built for the protection of farmers, woodcutters, fishermen and others whose temporary huts offered scant security against Indian raids, not to mention our sometime ruthless weather. This is borne out by the character of the buildings, whose exterior walls are of square-hewn logs of hard pine, ash or elm, usually seven or eight inches thick and strongly dovetailed at the corners. The log construction shows such careful workmanship that the spaces between the logs are often no more than an inch or two apart. In the larger of these houses, the second floor ceiling might be constructed in the 17th century manner with a "summer beam" supporting the floor joists.

Communities were often poor and remote. These log houses, and many of later date which still remain, possess little elaboration either of plan or architectural detail but have a character by which they achieve a great measure of spaciousness and dignity. Built altogether of wood by men who'd learned its qualities in building ships as well as houses, they show throughout a right use of the material.

The Original (**above**)
Stripping off the clapboard to reveal tremendous logs with a minimum of scaring from the strapping.

The Pre-build (**opposite page**)
Perfection is obvious as Bill Beaton starts to set up the walls. Only a fine wash will be needed to reveal the amazing color of the logs.

A common history, not overly dramatized, is somewhat representative of lives lived in a new land by courageous, hard-working families who use the material at hand for shelter and protection from natural elements, some of which lived on the land before them. The incredible amount of effort it took to erect four relatively impenetrable walls to create such a fortress-like structure was testament to their ingenuity and dedication to the safety of their community. The logs themselves tell their own long story in the countless rings that have witnessed every generation to settle the land since it first became a dream worth chasing. Such a house would speak to your soul of real memories, of true craftsmanship and the spirit of those who built it.

There was a deep pine forest, still to this day called Pine Valley, not too far north of Toronto, up near where Vaughn resides. To it came settlers quite enamored of those virgin timbers. They arrived with the ambition, expertise and tools to fashion the best log houses we've ever had the good fortune to find abandoned.

We set ourselves to collect these homes and therefore to restore them to their former glory, so they might serve other families who were bound to cherish them once again.

There was one in particular, the likes of which we had never seen. The fact that it had remained covered until we found it accounted in great measure for its condition. After we had removed its siding, we were aghast at the size of the logs. They were all hewn to a thickness of eight inches but the first one that sat upon the stone foundation, as I remember, was thirty inches tall. Those above it weren't much smaller. And the tight gaps between the logs wasted very little of the pine timber. I would have to admit, this was the best house of log we'd ever found after about forty years in the business. And for the next twenty years as well.

It came down cleanly and quickly, due to the fewer number of logs. Most houses of its size have ten or eleven courses to reach the usual height of about twelve feet. This one rivaled my first log house back in the sixties that had only six logs to reach that height. We erected it in our

The Show
Our best house taken to the New York log home show, including all windows, doors, mantelpiece, furniture and even an iron staircase.

The Set-up
In the middle of the arena we build the house with the help of a forklift. It's looking like a sure thing.

restoration yard but it didn't sell, probably because I'd put a premium price on it.

It was 1995, almost time for the big log home show in Charlotte, North Carolina in 1996. I thought I'd take a chance and enter this one in it, perhaps to show off I suppose. I'd shopped for them in the United States but I'd never seen one as good. I didn't see how it could miss. I planned on taking it with its windows and doors, all trimmed out with hardware, at least for the first floor.

I knew it could take a year to have them made. The second floor beams were monsters. So why not take half of them too? The summer beam would carry them to create a loft. Would I take a staircase too? That's when I thought of one of those classic metal spiral ones. There was a company in Toronto that made some beauties.

The trip wouldn't be cheap. I'd have to take at least four of us. And they must have forklifts. I'd have to arrange that. No, we'll need six. Les and Sarah would be good to have on the floor to do the selling. So that's what we did. It took a fifty-three footer to carry the load. We hoped it was a one-way trip.

After we all were set up in our hotel rooms, we went to check out the arena. It was certainly big enough. I was glad I reserved a big space in the center. Our load arrived the next morning, hitting a snag right off the bat. The truck couldn't get through the entrance doors. If we had to

The Barge (top)
Our client needed it on top of a cliff without road access. We barged the logs and a Telehandler across Lake Dorset.

Telehandler
This was the only machine that had the power and reach to get the heavy logs up to the top with minimum danger.

ngersoll Rand
VR-843C

Fireplace
A great place to show off some native art.

offload it outside, we'd be way behind other builders and have to navigate around them, and maybe lose our reserved forklift.

After everyone, including our hosts and the driver, spent much time agonizing about it, it was Sarah who came up with the solution. She suggested that air be let out of the tires. It was only an inch too tall, wasn't it? The plan worked!

I was surprised we were the only ones with a period log house. All the others were brand new, each with dubious methods of cornering and

Cabin?
Not your average cabin with monstrous logs like these, now nestled in a pine forest overlooking Lake Dorset.

Old Growth
Sean, a grown young man, is only a head taller than two old-growth timbers being put in their place for who knows how long?

Transoms
As if more light were needed, the huge transoms above the French doors could be opened for those lake breezes.

French Doors
There's easy access to the lakeside porch from the kitchen or living room with three sets of French doors to choose from.

Imagine
Wonder how tall that tree might have been, the one that carried over the three French doors.

insulating. Some, I would say, foolish. Once ours was up, it did receive a lot of praise and attention. After all, it was these originals that started the whole craze, as evidenced in this show. Only a few asked the price. It seems almost all came for the show, not to buy. I hadn't planned on taking it back home.

But that's what happened, even though we won a second place for best-in-show. First place had to go to the one that took center stage, a huge, walk-in ready to live-in house that must have cost the owner at least twenty-thousand to set up. We were all so disappointed, me most of all, having put another forty thousand into the move.

However, it was inevitable that someone would see the merit of this house. Nothing could ever match its magnificence. Along came the Delaneys. Jim was an orthopedic surgeon from Barrie who had a property on Lake Dorset in the eastern Muskokas that needed a great house. And that's what Jim and Sheila received.

When I eventually saw that his site was on top of a steep cliff, I had some real figuring to do. For sure, the entire load had to be barged to the site and it would have to be a big barge. Even then, getting it all to the top wouldn't be easy. I hoped a Telehandler was up to the job, one log at a time.

Well, there was a time when we almost lost the Telehandler and Joe our driver. I watched it rise up on two wheels in the mud, about to careen over the cliff. It hovered there for a few seconds as if wanting to go for a dive in the lake. Joe slowly shifted his weight to the other side to have it find purchase again. There were a few scary moments during the reconstructions but we got the building up until it reigned supreme over Lake Dorset.

Jim decided a log guesthouse would be in order, so we found one that suited, the kind with the usual size of logs, about ten to twelve inches in height per round. We fitted the place out with the correct windows and door as it deserved. Diminutive as it was, placed in close proximity to its statuesque neighbor, it was well-received and well-used over the years.

The house

# of six Sallys

Generations of family history are embedded in these stones, and a number of Sallys were part of it

Sally and Oliver
Proud parents with Simon on his first day of Junior Kindergarten.

The Thibideau stone house north of Cobourg was one of our more ambitious projects. This classic five bay Georgian house was resurrected from Forfar, a small village in eastern Ontario. It took me years of search then negotiation to finally purchase the building that, although built solidly of the local sandstone, a gorgeous creamy yellow, was not too far from dereliction. The magnificent interior certainly deserved saving.

I was quite impressed with the quality of the woodwork, obviously produced by a professional cabinetmaker.

It was later discovered that the original builder came from Rhode Island, which explained the quality of its design. American in manner and of excellent proportion throughout, it stood there where I first found it, showing off the many excellent details quite proudly. It had its returned eaves, thankfully all of its window trim, beautifully paneled doors, and paneled and canted window jambs. It even had its eyebrow and elliptical attic vents. I was not about to let this one get away. It eventually took me ten years of persistence.

Every care was taken to remove the whole lot as I intended to have every piece restored if necessary and put back just the way it was. The eventual plan added a pair of log cabins from the Ottawa valley, to be clad in a lovely butter-colored yellow clapboard and trim to tie it all together aesthetically.

This wasn't quite the puzzle that Marc and Robin thought it was going to be. Sure, it looked like that when you witnessed the broad field around the roughed-in frame of the central element of the house that stood amid an acre of stones just lying about like thousands of puzzle pieces, ready to be put in their proper place, one at a time. Yes, they were numbered but the numbers weren't needed. The stones were basically the same size, sort of like large loaves of bread but of different lengths, all easy stuff for good masons. And we had them, a piece of cake (or bread) in the hands of Ed and Wayne. We had the logsmiths too, who would build a log cabin at each end.

Research discovered that the stone building came with a name, The David Nichols House, and with quite a history at that, the narrative containing several interesting aspects. Prominent among these, and the cause of some confusion, is the fact there were four generations of David Nichols in the family, not to mention the inordinate number of Sallys that became part of its history.

One of them, albeit briefly, became involved in the great Mormon trek westward. Together with a number of relatives and friends, the Nichols joined the Mormon trek westward to the United States. Sarah (also known as Sally) had a brother, Arza Jr., born in Bastard Township in 1798, he'd first married Lucinda Adams, and later Jane Stoddard. Together, Arza and Jane went to North Dakota in a covered wagon, driven by oxen.

The story is told that Jane, on the long journey west, pointed to a large object in the field and asked her husband what it was.

When he told her it was a stone, she replied, "I thought we were never to see those again." The promised land was not to be found without its stones! But stones or not, the Azra Judds pressed on, eventually reaching

The Stones
It was a good thing we had lots of room for the stones on the site. We had enough from the basement to take the house up to a two story.

Leftover (opposite page)
After all was done, Ed got even more ambitious and used some leftover stones to make a grand archway, that found some purpose eventually.

their destination and remaining in the United States. But David and his wife Sally turned back, although we do not know how far they traveled. History confirms that they did return to Forfar from this escapade, but we do not know when exactly.

The David Nichols family arrived as emigrants from the United States c. 1800, purchasing the present property somewhere between the 1820s and 1830s. The first David Nichols, born in Rhode Island in 1730, with his wife Sally, may also have been the first of the family to arrive in Canada. They were listed in an 1804 census of Bastard Township as living here with their children, Ruth, Sheldon, Phoebe, Sally, David the third, Hiram, and an unnamed infant.

The present stone house, undoubtedly built by the third David, appeared on the Bastard Assessment Rolls for the first time in 1846. The family must have certainly been living in another building prior to this, most likely in the customary log dwelling. David and Sally were listed as being here by the time of the 1851 census.

When the Thibideaus sold the house, the new owner soon after asked me to design an English water garden to the west of the house. It was the large stone gate that Ed had erected from leftover stones that begged for a wall around the garden and it would hopefully, match the house. Where did they come from you might ask. Well, when we were taking down the Forfar house I realized the basement stones were the same and made sure to take them all, not really knowing if they would be needed at all. As it

turned out, they were, for two reasons. First, Marc and Robin wanted the house raised from a story-and-a-half to a full two-story. Fortunately, we had those stones from the basement to do that. Then, when the new owner needed a wall, we still had enough piled in the field to start it. Now this was to be a huge garden, about the size of a couple of tennis courts. It did not however, become the water garden I had designed for the space. It became a garden of rare trees and shrubs surrounded by a wall about five feet high of the same rare stones of yellow and cream. A roofed entertainment and barbecue stove was erected at one end of the garden and it is all quite spectacular!

So what next happened could never be guessed at. After all that, one of the most gracious, classical houses with two-hundred acres of grounds the like of which are seldom found, is being sold again. And who happens along to pick it up? Oliver and Sally.

Yes, you read it right, Sally. Is this a fairytale or what? Well, to Sally and Oliver it is, I suppose. They seem to be totally infatuated with everything about the house and property.

But then the story grew in crazy coincidences. Interestingly, the adjoining property to the northwest belonged to Bernie and Sally (not related to Oliver and Sally). The southwest property belonged to Allen and Sally (not related to Oliver and Sally). It seems the house and environs draws Sallys like bees to honey. The new mistress (the fourth owner) of the grand house and property is a Sally as well (our Sally, related to Oliver).

At the corner of their road, Oliver and Sally checked in at the Primrose Donkey Sanctuary and found a donkey they liked. Were they surprised to find it was named Sally (not related to Oliver and Sally)... yet.

And so ends the House of six Sallys... for now.

Gazebo (opposite page)
What's a garden without an outdoor place to barbecue and enjoy nature with friends? Come on and pick a hammock.

The Garden (opposite page)
The second owner asked me to design an English water garden. The third owner wanted the space for rare trees and shrubs. Voila!

The Game
Snooker anyone? Have a games room, a place to relax and have fun with friends and family.

FROM THE CURRENT OWNERS:

"In mid-2020, in the midst of the COVID-19 pandemic, we decided to take a drive to Roseneath to see a beautiful house on a beautiful property that Sally had seen listed online. We had lived in Toronto our whole lives and often went to open houses because of our mutual appreciation for architecture and design, but something felt very exciting about this visit even before we arrived.

From the moment we drove onto the property we knew that this was a very special place, and when we stepped into the house we instantly fell in love. It was a sunny August day and the warm breeze was blowing through the house — it was paradise! The attention to detail is incredible, the trim, the doors, the windows, the stone! Every room is more beautiful than the last. After spending a few hours in the house and touring the beautiful gardens and the rest of the property, we got back into our car

Arch (opposite page)
We carefully marked the stones that arched over the original gable entrance and put them back as they were.

Walkout
The best panoramic view over the lake is found off the master bedroom.

Solarium (following spread)
The spacious solarium serves family and guests in all seasons.

to drive back to the city, already longing to be back at the yellow house. At that moment we knew that this was where we wanted to raise our son Simon, and where we wanted to spend the rest of our lives.

We have been captivated by the house that we now call home and feel so grateful to have become friends with Mel. We love learning about the house's rich history (including having been home to several Sallys!) and about his experience of designing and building the home. The house is a true work of art, having been salvaged as three separate structures and combined into one to form such a beautiful space inside and out.

We love sharing the space with our friends and family including our new friends and neighbors who have warmly welcomed us to the community. We know we will always find it surreal when we look out over the fields and at the incredible sunsets we're so fortunate to experience. There's a real sense of detachment that we feel from our former selves and from our former lives in Toronto. It has been a blessing to relocate our lives to this beautiful place that we feel so deeply connected to."

— Sally Hood-Ranscombe and Oliver Pauk

A legacy born to live

"My father was born in a log house, so it seemed natural that we should live in one too," said Lois.

Antiques
Many of our clients gravitate naturally to the furnishings of yesteryear that are sometimes about the same age as the house, and looking like they came with the place.

Dining Room (opposite page)
The focal point being the fireplace with its promise of homemade baking right out of oven and served warm to the period hutch table.

Windsors (opposite page)
From my house to the Kuebler's house, came the c. 1780 set of seven red Windsor chairs.

I suppose when they saw the article in *Century Home* that featured one of the log homes we'd built, they were hooked on the idea. But Lois and Conrad Kuebler had to admit to a log home generational history.

"My father was born in a log house and it seems strangely fitting that we too should have a log home," says Lois, pointing to the small log cabin in the framed picture on the wall.

"And we honeymooned at the Chateau Montebello log lodge too. Somehow, it just felt right." said Conrad.

Well, their home may have started with a cabin. I think the smaller of the two we put together was a blacksmith's shop, probably about eighteen or twenty by twenty-six, if I remember.

The other one was larger, helping to create a family size dwelling with what was looking like a four-bedroom. We planned it together carefully, agreeing easily on the division of space. It took on an L shape that basically gave access to the right or left from either the first or second floor once you entered from the stone-clad Georgian entrance with sidelights

and transom. You would then encounter a bit of drama right away, finding yourself in a vaulted space from floor to roof ridge.

A staircase with winders at the bottom took you upstairs to a loft of bedrooms, the master with its en-suite taking the entire floor to the west and three various-sized bedrooms for what would probably be various-sized kids to the east wing. The first floor of the larger log house, of course, became the kitchen and dining room with a three-piece bath off the kitchen. The Kuebler house, I was glad to know, may have been the only one we've built with a period-style fireplace with bake oven that was actually regularly used. Lois was very adept at dishing up cookies, buns or bread, doing it the old way, which somehow tasted better, as expected. We do however, include the modern amenities, blending the past and present; lacking nothing in modern living while preserving the ambiance of earlier times.

Foyer
From the foyer; left to kitchen and dining room; right to living room and up the winding stair to three bedrooms and baths.

Exterior choices of material have been well known and well used for a long time in Canada. Cedar shingles on the roof, board and batten pine (sometimes stained or painted), for gable ends and additions, small-paned windows and stone chimneys, all combine to enhance the appearance of a period log home. This was the pattern I set, I suppose when I used them on my first country home. When visitors came to our antique shop the odd one would admire the log house and realize they wanted to live in one like that. The next thing I knew, that's what I was building for others… if I could find them.

When it came time to think about where to put the garage there were obstacles to deal with. The creek (or small river to be more accurate) was one challenge and getting a bridge over it another. And a flat spot for the garage was quite a way from the house. The eventual solution was a departure for sure — under the house. It was the grade that decided it. You could drive right in with no problem at all. That's not to say it was easy to build… it wasn't, needing for one thing, a completely sealed and well-insulated floor to the upstairs.

The Master
The spacious master bedroom was graced with the splendid stitchery by Lois for the pencil post bed.

I was happy to see how naturally Lois and Conrad had come to appreciate antiques. Though it was new to them they were studious and almost relentless in their pursuit of them, realizing not only the aesthetic appeal but also their ability to establish an authenticity to the period home that it may not otherwise have. Early on I suggested they take in a couple of the antique shows that offered up the choice pieces. When they attended an early Bowmanville show with Jean and I, I was surprised that when I pointed out three or four of the best pieces (for beauty, authenticity and investment), they secured them all for the house. Their collection grew from that to beautify their log home. They certainly were a great couple to work with.

The seven-

bay beauty

The pieces in a drive shed became a labor of love for Barry and Karen

I've known Ray Smith for a long time. It goes back to the early years of antique collecting when, with the help of a few antiquarians, our true antiques survived the fad of stripping furniture, in some measure at least. We fought to preserve the original finish and colors that gave them the character their owners bestowed on them.

We'd often meet at the best antique shows held in Canada. That's not many but it was the few that showed off the "good stuff." I had just visited him and was pleased to see not only the few "old friends" he got from me but the wonderful collection he'd amassed over the years. The facts took their time to stitch together, or pull apart, rather like the tangled wool of a weed-ravaged lamb. This is the consequence of age, Ray and I each a fragile bookend on either side of our eightieth year. So with some dedication, all we antiquarians can do is retrieve the stories that come with each house before we are gone like the passenger pigeons.

I was there to confirm a few of the facts regarding the house from Jerseyville that I'd bought from him back in the late eighties. I first saw its disassembled parts, stored away in the barn behind his stone house that sat amid his flock of sheep that he lovingly tended as their shepherd.

Foyer (right and opposite page) There's something about a double-door entrance that's very inviting — and convenient too. You would only open them both for a herd or the new refrigerator.

The Van Sickle house came from Jerseyville, a small town not far east of Guelph. The road through it was an old indian trail that wound down from Dundas and Ancaster to Brantford. The Van Sickles eventually came down this trail from Missouri, probably as United Empire Loyalists. The Howells, the other side of the family, perhaps UELs as well, came from New Jersey. Incidentally, Ray showed me a pewter plate with the Van Sickle family history that had been taped on its back for who knows how many years. He'd found it accidentally while searching for antiques in Mary Page's antique shop in New Hampshire. Perhaps the plate had fallen off the covered wagon as it jerked along its long rocky journey from the old homestead.

Portico (**below and opposite page**) Doug Vickers, a fine cabinetmaker, was enlisted by Barry to reproduce the wide portico that really dressed up the front exterior.

The Plate Inspecting the pewter plate's engraving with care, we found the date 1786 and a family history.

So how did Ray secure this treasure of a house, you might be asking? Well, the story that came to me was that the owner, devastated by a house fire and the loss of a brother, was at odds as to the future of the house and its upkeep. There were a few interested parties, but it was only Ray who promised the owner a complete restoration. That was the key that would unlock the door to allowing it to live again. They found agreement and the building, as it stood, was his. He then found someone competent to disassemble the house, taking care to avoid breakage and to get every piece of it into his barn. Fortunately, the immense task was completed successfully.

One particularly artistic feature of the house was its stenciled walls — Ray had every intention of preserving them as best as possible. Much research and experimentation was applied to the task. The answer, not without considerable difficulty, involved a heavy layer of fiberglass applied to the back of the wood lath to stabilize each panel that was to be preserved. This, being attempted in the winter before the house was to come down, meant that the work had to be done alongside the generator that ran the heater to cure the fiberglass and keep the workers from freezing. Ray also traced each element of the art and made mylar stencils that could come in handy later for touch-ups or repairs.

Garden (below and opposite page)
A view of a well-organized door garden through a classic twelve over twelve window.

Ray had thought to rebuild the house on an acquired annexation of his property but was delayed by a ruling that would disallow its reconstruction until that section of land had been owned for five years.

In the interim, Ray's affairs were in flux, to put it mildly. Unfortunately, Ray did not have the means to carry the project further. Somehow, the house came to my attention and I went to Ray's place to have a look.

He was correct to suspect that I might be one to carry the ball, so to speak. This was right up our alley, restoration being what my company had been doing since the sixties. We started out finding log houses that were worth restoring but didn't turn a blind eye to other modes of building. There were those magnificent barns that always impressed with their hand-hewn beams. I think over the years we'd turned about six of them into spectacular homes. There was one post-and-beam built home that became my own — after years of restoration. Then there were the stone houses too that often needed help. We couldn't pass them by.

So here we were again, confronted by what appears to be one of the great examples of architecture of the early 18th century. I was astounded at what I'd found but not surprised at the perception of Ray in realizing the evident quality and rarity of this home.

Almost as soon as I bought it from Ray, Barry Ezrin, an antique dealer in the area, was my first potential buyer. In a way, I was reticent to part with it, anticipating the glory hidden in that barn that could be brought to fruition. In all my years studying Ontario's early architecture, I had never seen a seven-bay Georgian house with such a promise of period integrity. I'm guessing Barry and Karen hadn't either.

Stencils (opposite page)
It was Ray who found a way to salvage the stencils. Fiberglass on the wood lath was the key to stabilizing them so they could come out in large sections.

This pewter platter belonged to Margaret Whitesell who married a ? They were Father and Mother to Sarah

Montgomery ? who married ? Howell. Sarah Howell was their daughter, she married Abram Van Sickle.

The church

on the hill

From bell tower
to blossoms in flower
it becomes a place
that embraces all
with grace

Jim and Kathryn Calladine drove onto my property in their pure white Lotus Elan, a beautiful, low-slung sport car. I was surprised that the driver managed to get out of it, given his stature. They had just parked in front of the gate to the house when their Lotus sort of exploded in a cloud of smoke.

It sure looked like it was a goner, at least a very expensive repair. They didn't seem as distraught as I would have thought as they stood, seemingly transfixed, staring at the huge log walls of the house.

I invited them in of course, knowing they may need to call for CAA or someone. I offered to tow them into Uxbridge if they had no other recourse. But they were more interested in the house than their car. Evidently, they were searching the local roads for a property, hoping to vacate Toronto, possibly permanently. Jim began to question me thoroughly in order to understand what was necessary in order to have a house like ours for themselves.

Jean and Kathryn were getting along famously. I soon realized they had a dream and a certain focus on its eventuality.

Jim explained that his travel company, Calladine and Baldry, was taking too much of his time and he and Kathryn needed a place in the

country to get away to. I was surprised that after much discussion, that we had mutual friends. We had just built a stone house reproduction for their friends Tom and Helen Morley south of town. They loved the land around them, hoping to find something like their friends had.

I immediately realized how great it would be to build again so close to home. When I mentioned the log church from Sundridge that I'd just acquired they both got very excited. That's often how it happens. It's a kind of serendipity, things just coming together when they're needed.

As luck would have it, as it does for some, a two-hundred acre parcel came up for sale just one road over from the Morleys. Jim didn't hesitate and secured it. Not long after the deed was transferred, they came back to have a design started that would turn a church into a home. Actually, I never thought them so dissimilar in purpose. We took time to go over the site to find the best place for the house. There was a hill at the back of the property that would have a view over everything to the west. The fact that the road through the property to the preferred site would be a mile long didn't seem to deter Jim. I had to guess that they really wanted to get away. At the time, I had a large inventory of cobblestones that I thought would look good from the grade to the first log, a short stone wall that varied from two to three feet high. It was a good start.

The structure itself offered many interesting features. The main space would become the Great Room that would soar all the way to the roof. A back-to-back fireplace would taper all the way up, offering a large hearth to the Great Room with the other servicing the dining room. An upper bedroom (also with a fireplace) would have a balcony overlooking the room below. Of course the eleven foot gothic windows brought a distinguished quality of light into that large room. All concerned thought that a bell tower might be in order as well!

An addition was planned for a large kitchen and a back-to-back staircase accessed from both the main hall or from the kitchen for Kathryn to get to her private darkroom. Another two bedrooms and a pair of bathrooms completed the preliminary design.

Jim had a requirement that I wouldn't be much help with. He wanted windmill power to power the house. He found a company that would put

Vistas (opposite page)
With the house settling on a hill over two hundred acres, it was hard not to be dazzled by the vistas everywhere about.

The Crew
It was a wonderful crew of guys, interested in their craft and eager to produce good work. Many went on to create their own companies years later.

Windows (above and following page)
Unusual for us, to have Gothic windows to reproduce for a log house, especially the seventeen footer for the kitchen and Kathryn's photo studio above it. The circular one in the bell-tower gable was a test too, for sure.

Chimney (below right)
Master mason, Glen Ward, lights the first fire in his triple firebox fireplace.

in the two poles and windmills. My guys did work hard to get the twelve locomotive storage batteries into the basement. In the end, it turned out that there wasn't enough wind on this hill. Hydro was contracted to do their thing after all.

Over the summer, the house seemed special to everyone involved. I wondered how accidental it was to have a minister (I forget which faith but perhaps Mormon or Mennonite), who was also a master carpenter, to be foreman over the job... for the rebuilding of a church, of all things. It may have been one of the reasons it went so well. We finished the job by building a two-car saltbox garage.

I should mention that we also built a great friendship that has lasted to this day.

An afternoon after the house sat proudly on the top of the hill I wrote this:

THIS HOUSE
This house, a lofty sentinel
sits above the valley below the clouds
that part to let the sun beat down approvingly.
Majestic it stands, this monument,
firmly fixed into the earth from which it came.
Not long before it was a seed
that journeyed through our mind,
borne aloft by our imagination,
our will the weight to press it home.
Its root goes down beneath our time,
a well that gives up dignity.
No stranger here, its friends the sun,
the moon, the winged and wingless
fly and frolic in its shadow.
As children beneath her skirt
she lifts us up to her, embracing us,
her folds become our own.
This grace bestowed, we thus inherit
a legacy that's laid, a cornerstone
that's set in love, the mortar of the soul.

Meant for

each other

The timber "sisters" from the Ottawa Valley and the young couple dreaming of a log home

I remembered two log houses from the Ottawa Valley. They each seemed somewhat forlorn where they stood alone in a barren field. They were approximately the same size and would each be quite able to house a small family comfortably. The fact that neither had that responsibility at the moment, may have accounted for their current melancholy.

Well, I do dislike homes that suffer the fate of abandonment. Having found them independently but within the span of a moon's quarter, I took some meaning of this and considered introducing them to each other in our yard where we often restore homes to their once-fulfilled selves. Perhaps, as we attended to their incidental external blemishes, they came to realize that their fates were not fated for separation after all.

One would have to admit, they were becoming a very inviting pair when seen together, seemingly standing in anticipation of life together.

It was about that time that the Focklers were feeling that they needed something more substantial to care for their family. They took the time to visit the site, to size up these walls of hand-hewn log for trustworthiness and, I supposed, to explore their own potential for loving this style of house that was so unfamiliar to them.

Allowing the two couples time to greet each other, I went to the car to get some rough plans I had sketched up to show them a few ways to marry the two houses together. After a while, they came back smiling. That was always a good sign in my estimation.

The Focklers liked it well enough to commit to the pair of houses, hoping to start a foundation (according to my plan) in the following spring. I guess they thought the "sisters" were meant for them.

Ken Fockler was an executive at IBM, and like many of the city-bound, dreamt of a possible life with his family in the country not too far from Toronto. He and his wife, Nancy, worked closely with me to design that dream for them. When I showed them my favorite method for putting the two houses together, they seemed to love the idea immediately.

The key was to add a stone entrance between them as the main entrance with sidelights and a transom to light the foyer. Being centered between the houses, a stairway off the foyer allowed access to bedrooms upstairs — some being in one house to the left, probably for the kids, with the parents in the other house to the right. They liked that idea too. I mentioned that the added theme of stone should be carried on in the form of exterior walls for the fireplaces and a short curtain wall from the grade to the base logs, all to tie it together visually. Right off the bat, they got right into it. Once the plan was finalized, Ken started to cut the pieces that would become the small (not so small as it turned out) doll-house model for their daughter. He was surprised at how much material it took, given the size he chose. It put one in mind of the unbelievable number of square feet of lumber that the full size house would consume, not to mention the labor to assemble it all into an adults' family home.

Of course the daughter was enchanted with her new toy and, in her way I suppose, helped to build it (i.e. where her room would be and just how big her toy closet would be). Ken even painted the logs on the exterior walls as well as placing the windows and doors to the scale shown on

the final plans for the grown-ups. He even painted the window and door trim to everyone's preferred color, a pretty bright red. The rooms were portioned accordingly, the model suggesting a few changes for the better. There was some debate about whether to separate the dining room from the kitchen. Someone won out, deciding on the separate room. They liked my idea of a Dutch door going out to the balcony that hung out over the walkout below. It was agreed to clad the basement walkout with the same stone as would be used for the two chimneys rising up through the gable ends and through the roof.

I personally built the cherry cupboards and counter for the kitchen while John, our best cabinetmaker, built the staircase off the foyer, which was big enough to accept a generous two-piece bath on the west wall.

When Ken and Nancy saw pictures of some of the fireplaces we've built, Nancy in particular focused on one that had a working bake oven on the side of it. She wanted one like that, thinking it a great feature for their house. The kitchen, however, was too small a room for it so we planned to have it in the north wing, which would be the main living room. An eight-foot wide wall of brick was required to house the oven, including a twelve-by-twelve hand-hewn pine beam for a lintel, the underside and interior surface being asbestos board to pass code.

Dollhouse (previous spread)
It's true Ken started the (large) miniature house but the daughter took charge when it came to where her room would be and how big to make her toy closet.

Guest House (previous spread)
As usual, when most was accomplished, the idea of a guest house came up. If I had one, a spot was found for it.

It took a few weeks in the spring to amass the quantity of stone required, not just for the chimneys but the curtain wall that surrounded the entire structure between grade and the sill logs. The walkout itself took hundreds of large stones alone. We decided on a sandstone that was found locally. This added a lot of interesting color to good effect.

Alas, none of us ever had time to take advantage of either of the two great features on the other side of their road. The Devil's Paintbrush and The Devil's Pulpit were both excellent golf courses right across their road. And the twenty-five acre property they were settling on was riddled with great trails that opened up to wonderful fields further up the hill. So, no time for recreation. But we weren't here for that. We were here to help realize a dream... for Ken and Nancy.

Built before

Fort York

...and to this day,
a treasured
Riverdale residence

Acoustics (above)
Turns out a log house has good acoustics for music-makers. I've been there when they're doin' the blues and it sounds good to me.

Beamwork
When it came time to carry a second floor, we needed some big beams. I happened to have them but who'd fit the joists? Our lady carpenter accomplished the task with expertise.

Stair
Without an exterior wall, there's no wall long enough to take a staircase. Skilled carpenter Maarten Bomers took many hours to create the curves for this winding staircase, a showpiece in this old house.

Counter
Hey, this paneled wainscoting might fit. There's four of them. And with great original graining too. I can see them now in the kitchen.

After the big storm, I got a tip to check out a damaged house up near a small hamlet called Osaka. No, I didn't have to go to Japan to find it. It was in Ontario, not far from Toronto. A house that once was, but not anymore. The big maple tree in the yard had crushed the place in two when it fell. A lightning strike most likely. Good thing it was abandoned. The log house was obviously built in the last century, the kind I'm always looking for. Unfortunately, they are becoming quite scarce now.

This endeavor could give me quite a few more spare logs, the kind that I always need. Going through the debris, I took time to measure the structure's original footprint. It was the a bit bigger than most, about thirty-two by twenty-six, so I will find many logs to recycle into one of my projects. Then I noticed that the damage took out one side of the house more than the other. I instantly thought of the left side as a small bunky. They were popular as fun houses for the kids or even a small garage.

I'd better take it all with me, I concluded. Later, I was able to re-erect three walls that would measure twenty-six on the long side by about sixteen on the two short sides. I'd have to wait for the material of the fourth side. In the meantime, I had put it up as a display piece on the edge of town with a phone number in easy view. That, at least, put the wall to some use. Not long after it stood there I got a call from Don Procter, who would like me to see his and his wife's house in the Riverdale area of Toronto. He thought he and Bev might have a use for it. It turned out they lived on Broadview Avenue, overlooking the park, the one I used to toboggan down when I was a kid.

The house was of the stuccoed Regency style but it had a history more interesting than its exterior revealed. It was a log house, purported to be one of the earliest homes in Toronto. He showed me the remains of an old foundation that perhaps carried a lean-to kitchen. Then came the serendipitous fact of the matter. I measured it to be about twenty-six by sixteen with the exterior of their house exposed as log. Not only that, but they were about the same size of log as in my three-walled relic.

We all instantly knew this was too good to be true. Needless to say, we got into the planning that languished in the mysterious depths of

Serendipity
How come these old logs for the kitchen wing are about the same size as the original ones used to build the main house?

the Toronto bureaucrats who, it seems, had never had an historic log house (should we say relic) added to something before. Once this hurdle was passed, however, the relic found its purpose as a kitchen to its mother house.

The house soon became popular with Canadian movie producers who took advantage of the historic country home that sat so close to the core of the city. It became the set of period dramas and even a horror movie. The Procters and I became good friends, taking on another challenge twelve years later with the city planners, designing an upper floor above the kitchen.

It seems Don and Bev were destined to own a heritage home. They had read an article in the *Globe and Mail* about a previous owner of the home, who while ripping out some drywall to repair a leak, exposed the hidden log wall. They had to check it out for themselves. They were surprised to find a For Sale sign in the snow drift on the lawn.

Sometime after they were happily ensconced in their new home, they decided something should be done to replace the dilapidated extension on the back of the house.

It was twenty-three years ago now when they came to see me in Port Hope. The three-sided log house I had in inventory not only matched the size of the logs in their house but fit the old foundation perfectly. Convincing the city that it warranted a building permit however, was another

The Movies
If you're producing a movie in Canada, where do you go for your period sets? Not far if you can, when it's cheaper to work near home. So that's why they use that old house on Broadview Avenue.

matter. "We don't build log in the city," was their immediate response. Bev took the plans and the matter into her own hands, setting off into officialdom in high heels and a grim determination. She came back with a building permit. Maybe it was her bursting into tears in front of the administrator that did it.

The extension became a cosy and modestly furnished kitchen. "The heating bills are nothing," comments Don. "There's a radiator in the room but it's rarely used. The logs provide excellent insulation."

Don and Bev have been careful with further updates and modifications to the house, taking great care to preserve the historical integrity of the building. When a living room window needed replacement, they hired a heritage craftsman from Niagara who could meet the 19th century standards typical in the house. "You could say there are several evolutions of history in this house," said Don, while standing in his approximately 200-year-old living room.

Stair
It's not mid-century modern ... yet.

History: The John Cox cottage at 469 Broadview Avenue, Toronto, a log cabin-turned Regency cottage still resides on its original site. The United Empire Loyalist, John Cox erected the original dwelling on a 270 acre stretch of land east of the Don River in the late 1700s or early

1800s. The first stage of the structure was a small 16 x 24 feet log cabin facing due south and was completed no later than 1807, making it arguably older than the Gibraltar point Lighthouse and the various barracks at Fort York.

The walls containing the living room, including the external south wall and half the west wall, plus half the internal east wall separating the kitchen and living room, remain concealed original log; while the northern parts were expanded during a very early Victorian renovation. Some of the original square cut logs from the east wall, looking remarkably like the neighboring scalding cabin, are still visible from inside the recent rear kitchen addition. The kitchen addition itself has kept up with the spirit of the house, built using logs from a carefully disassembled "younger" log cabin (circa-1840). The original attic with its cedar roof still survives under the later Victorian roof and is visible from inside the house.

The Ghost
There's a ghost in the attic even older than they think, a secret attic lost in two hundred years of darkness.

The silk purse

A kiss of color livens up a remote country home restoration

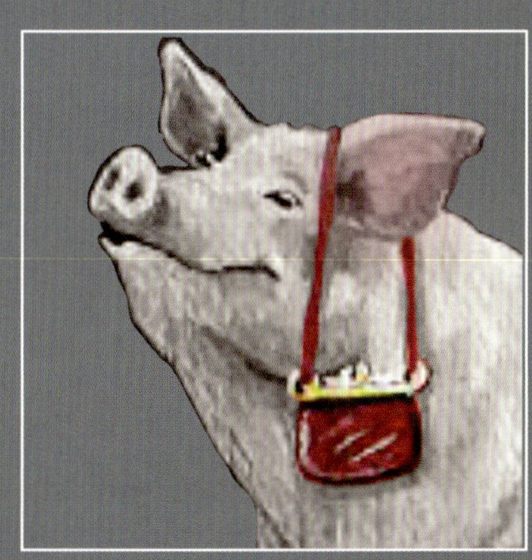

The Ceiling
It was a joke, this thing that was supposed to hold up the second floor. A cat would fall through it and die in the debris beneath. So we added a mighty beam and nice big hand-hewn floor joists.

It was not the usual reason I was driving the dump road. For one thing, I was far from the route to my own dump near Port Hope. I was surprised at the beautiful establishments on this road however, near Campbellford. I was following the lead from a realtor to what sounded like a nice three acre property. I thought it time to seek out a private place, perhaps for a small getaway cabin later. As I arrived up the hill to encounter the entrance, I was pleased with the outlook and the mature trees on the lane. The realtor mentioned that there was an old house on the property but not worthy enough to affect the price of the land.

It was a log house I was surprised to find, something I am more than familiar with, having restored countless of them. The realtor was right. It was not a worthy subject, so past its prime, if it ever had one. I had to admit, whoever built the structure put it on the right spot to take advantage of the view, about where I would put something, maybe even another log house that better deserved the spot. I did buy the property, in anticipation of some future here.

My crew and I arrived somewhat later to determine a quick way to extricate the house without making a mess of the road or surrounding terrain. A quick inspection would help plan a way to do the job. It had a foundation of sorts which, we supposed with some shoring up here and there, could accommodate another structure. Of course the bottom logs

The Fireplace
It was a gift actually. You never find a center fireplace in an old wreck of a log house. And finding a period mantle that fit the opening that was another gift.

Décor
Walls in early years were whitewashed, today painted white sometimes, to lighten the rooms.

were shot, much as we find most log homes we attempt to recover. The ceiling joists were a joke, obviously someone's mistaken idea of helping to keep the second floor up. We had to avoid going up there altogether. The rafters weren't much better, explaining the sway-backed roof. Most of the chinking had fallen out, partly because it hadn't been wired in. A house built before wire was invented? Wouldn't surprise me.

"We could fix this one up you know," said someone behind me. Was I hearing right? It was Ed, who always has a good grasp of a situation when confronted with a new challenge. "I can only see about six logs we'd have to replace. And the cement chinking would all be taken out in a couple of hours. We're lucky there's no wire. Getting that out's what so time-consuming. And new two-by-twelve rafters would give you a good roof when packed with lots of insulation."

"And didn't I see some nice hand-hewn joists in the yard? That'd take care of the second floor. Heck, I could have that old ceiling down this afternoon." That was Joe. I sort of believed him. But did I want the

expense? It was usually the client who paid our way through such work. It was Ed again who may have convinced me.

"Surely it'd be cheaper to fix this one than to build a new house, wouldn't you think?" And then Les came back from checking out the dilapidated drive shed.

"I know it looks bad but it's not really that far gone. We just have to straighten up the plates and wall beams and recover with board and batten."

"And how often do you find a center chimney almost ready to go? What would that cost? It probably only needs a chimney sweep. I guess I was coming around. They're probably right. It was at about this time that fate did us a favor. There was an unsightly broken down barn on the property that was certainly beyond use. I couldn't spare the man-hours to do anything with it. We returned from a weekend to find the smoldering ashes of the beams and refuse that had caught fire, clearing the area quite nicely. There was no evidence of vandals or trespassing. As I remember seeing paper litter and glass all over its floor, I determined it was spontaneous combustion. No kidding. Was this a sign?

Fine Ingress
It is almost impossible to find a nice entrance these days, the kind with transoms and sidelights. Back then though, we found not one, but two. Front and back, both beauties.

Kitchen
Just as an afterthought, a shingled kitchen wing with exposed rafters and a heated floor with a Dutch door too.

So, after all avenues were debated and chosen, we divided up the jobs and proceeded in the way most usual for us, carefully and methodically removing the unwanted, weak and/or rotten pieces while leaving what's left in a stable condition and ready for a do-over. We were part way into the work, gratified with our progress. It was looking possible that some worthiness was forthcoming after all so I ordered new windows, making sure that the log openings were trimmed to a common size for easy fitting. Once the log plates were spaced and leveled, the new rafters were hammered into place. I was very fortunate to find not one but two front and back entrances with sidelights and transoms. They were available back then but were now very scarce. The pair dressed up the house immeasurably. I even found a nice simple mantle in original red that fit the chimney breast perfectly. It seemed all this was meant to be.

But, perhaps not for me.

Word got out about the restoration and inquiries came requesting its availability, price, etc. Consequently, it just so happened that future work in distant parts would not give me time to take advantage of the lovely site as I had hoped.

A Mr. John Silberg ventured up the lane one day to see what we were doing. It was when we were beginning to cover the logs with thick insulation batts. This he found most curious. It did not however, dissuade him from further inspection. I explained that I intended to cover the whole exterior with board and batten and have it painted a color yet undecided. He invited me back to his house to meet his wife and consider the possibility of them having it for themselves. They lived in a very nice, well-appointed house and I found myself wondering why they would choose to trade it for what I had been calling "Westwind."

I had loaned a few of my architectural books to the Silberg's that they found interesting, giving them ideas they might employ themselves. In particular, the whitewashed interiors of the logs would brighten up things considerably while creating a good canvas for their painted antique furnishings.

I did not discourage their ambition. My costs to restore the house included a complete new exterior façade for the log house and a restoration of the driveshed. We agreed on a price and it would soon be theirs.

Staircase
Getting upstairs in a log house is sometimes tricky. There's often a window or door in the way of a stair. It can be done if winders are allowed. They take up less space too.

The coast-to-

coast cape

An east-coaster tells its personal tale while crossing a vast continent

The Stop
Many a tired traveler frequented it, probably on horseback. But come what may, the horse was replaced and the old inn was lost in the dust of a faster future.

I think it was the Killams that tipped off the Campbells that I had a Cape in inventory. It seems that Janet and Bill Campbell, but Janet in particular, was infatuated with the style. Janet always pictured a house with those simple, unadorned lines gracing their Gulf Island meadow. She never fully realized the possibility until coming to me for the real thing.

I have only had one other and it was quite exceptional, having its entire interior intact. To find those wide, beaded wall boards covering all interior walls and ceilings was more than I'd ever hoped for. It sits now on a lovely fifty-acre tract of land near Gravenhurst Ontario, put back together as it always was, looking like it grew there. But that's another story.

The one I have now came from Elmsdale Nova Scotia and was once a stagecoach stop in the late 18th century. I'm sure it's seen its share of weary travelers and taken care of them well. Now however, I wouldn't be surprised if it was feeling lonely without something to do.

"Well, you're right about that, I could tell you, if anybody'd care to listen," responded the Cape. "There I was, sitting comfortably, gazing out at the ocean through my many windows, taking in the calm but sometimes stormy sea, the vigils entering my rooms for so many days and nights I could never count them. What am I going to do? It's lonely with no one to take care of. I always have this empty feeling ... and unwanted. Surely there must be some family that needs me. All I have is my views of the water that gives me some peace. I can always gaze out at the ocean and wait and wonder what will become of me. I may be old but I am wise in the way of caring. Oh me, oh my. What am I to do?"

Then, from out of nowhere, a crescendo of mechanical noise surrounds the sad old Cape.

"What's going on? What's all that noise? It sounds like hammering. Ouch! It feels like my roof is coming off. I'm being violated. It feels like I'm being taken apart. That can't be. Leave me alone. I live here. I've always lived here. Now something is picking at my bones. But I have to stay together. Don't do this to me. Leave me alone. But I can't get away; I know that. I've always known that. I'm rooted here. Moving is impossible. I have to wait here for someone to find me."

Without the cape realizing (of course), the old pole rafters are being picked off the wall plates ever-so-carefully. They are being numbered as usual. Then somewhere else, the old worn out shingles that have withstood so many decades of ocean-side wind and rain are being stripped off the exterior. They are taken away, never needing to serve again. Now the windows can come out. This is done with care, avoiding breakage as best as possible so they can be reused.

"Oh no... not my views. I am lost without them. Put them back! They are my world out there... the world to me. They are my eyes. I would be blind. Don't do this to me. Please. No!"

Now the mighty hand-hewn posts and beams that have kept the Cape erect, fit and true forever in its life are exposed. They too are carefully numbered.

"This is terrible. I'm feeling strange indeed. I don't ever remember feeling... I don't know what to call it... naked? I don't like that at all. Stop it! Put it back. Put me all back." To its total astonishment, the views were gone. It was like the darkest night... and the Cape was blind.

Then the pins that held the many post and tie-beams together were hammered out so that each could be carefully pulled apart and laid down in a proper order for easy numbering and proper removal. The floorboards were next to be pried off the basement joists. They too were numbered so they could be returned to their always place. It was soon all ready to be loaded for the trip.

After much more mechanical noise, the Cape is moving.

"Ouch! What's happening? I'm being bounced around. That hurts. Am I going somewhere? This is so disturbing. I can't tell up from down."

Unfortunately, the Cape was not able to avail itself of the views it might otherwise have enjoyed, being lashed down in a tight waterproof

bundle. Mind you, it might not have been interested anyway, there not being any oceans to observe as the large flatbed made its way through vast plains and mountain passes. No, it could only dream its favorite dream, of sharing some shore with someone it could care for as it was born to do.

After what seemed an incredibly long time, the noise and the movement stopped. The Cape could have sworn (although it did not have the inclination or the means to do so), that it was floating. It was a very nice feeling after all the jerking around it was subjected to. Almost as calming as it used to be when sitting on its own foundation. Then suddenly, the Cape found itself being picked apart and strewn all over the place. That was disturbing enough but what really pricked its senses was the smell. Yes, of course the Cape had senses. What did you think? It was inanimate? That smell was ingrained in every fiber of its being. It was the ocean. Did it matter that it wasn't its ocean? Not one bit. It was slightly different but not enough to be displeasing. The Cape absorbed the invigorating essence of it. And when its sill beams were being laid out on the beach, he felt the sand as a welcoming friend.

Among the crowd that were trying to make sense of all of the parts laying about, were two people who seemed to be more excited than the others. The Cape dared to think who they might be. It heard the man call out a name to another. It sounded an awful lot like Janet. The Cape had good ears, as do all houses. Yes, over the many, many years it had witnessed so many dramas, never once considering it to be eavesdropping, but perhaps it was. When the woman named Janet came closer to examine all the wonderful parts of the Cape, the Cape felt something it hadn't felt for a long, long time — that she and her family may be the ones that it could shelter for the rest of their lives, as they shared this oceanfront together.

A bachelor's

cozy den of log

It started on
a honeymoon...
someone else's

Shelley and I were now finally boarding our Air Canada flight to Mexico. This time, instead of hitch-hiking all over it, as per usual, the travel amenities had been upgraded to celebrate our honeymoon in a somewhat finer style. After taking in a few things in Zihuatanejo, we took a taxi to Ixtapa, where I got a great deal at the Las Brisas — two weeks for the price of one.

Shelley took the window seat with her hubby (me) close beside. Once we were airborne we started to relax. I supposed everyone on board, since it was June, may be honeymooning too. The fellow sitting next to me, it turned out, was going to the very same hotel. I couldn't help but notice he was reading one of those in-plane magazines from the seat pocket in front of him. With even a quick squint at his page, it seemed familiar to me. I thought I saw the distinctive artwork of a friend of mine. Sure enough, when I reached for the same magazine in front of me and turned to the same page, I was right. It was John Richmond's drawing and the article was about historic log houses which, by the way, also featured the builder of them, me, the guy sitting right beside the stranger.

It wouldn't be the first time I came across a magazine article about our work. The architectural journalists always seemed to be on the lookout for interesting projects to write up. Once, I was browsing the magazine aisle and picked up a copy with quite a nice cover. I thought to myself, that's just about the way I would have done it. Then, when I opened up the article it all came back to me. Yes, that's Robin and Mark's house that I designed and built about ten years ago, north of Cobourg. That became about the thirtieth magazine article in my collection. Of course, I'm pleasantly surprised each time I happen across them. This sure is a strange way to find one though, in the backseat of a 707, a few miles above the Pacific Ocean. I'm not kidding. A quick scan of the article proved, as expected, that John wrote in over-the-top terms about my artistic approach to architectural design and the many advantages of living in a period log home of the early 19th century. I casually asked the fellow, while he held the same article, "Do you like log houses too?" He looked over immediately.

"I sure do. That's what I want some day soon."

"Really?" I said, "That's interesting. Maybe I could help you. I'm Mel Shakespeare."

He looked shocked. And why wouldn't he? You can't generally conjure up such happenstances. It was as though he'd made a mental note of the name on the page. He had to consult the magazine again to check the name he'd just read. He became very excited when he finally believed me. I think I even had to show him my driver's license.

He then introduced himself to Shelley and I as Bruce Livingston who lived near Erin, Ontario. We were soon into a great conversation. Yes, he was staying at the same hotel. Yes, he was serious about having a follow-up about this but not until after the vacation, perhaps during the flight back. And yes, he was on the same flight back.

The day before leaving, we had a lunch with John to confirm his phone and address so we could keep in touch. Bruce passed us a large bag, a gift he said, mentioning that we should open it later in our room.

It turned out to be a big bag of pot. Well as much as we might have enjoyed it, I could not inhale pot due to a weak lung. Shelley had an idea though. She said she'd brew up a tea with it. Why not? We sipped the tea with little effect and gave it no more thought, going off to buy presents for ourselves and others at home. We collected quite a hoard of goodies, stopping off for an enjoyable lunch in a nice restaurant before our boarding time.

We jumped up suddenly when we heard our names called to our flight, desperately running to make it just in time. After we were seated in the plane we both had the same scary realization.

"Where's our stuff?" We'd left everything, about two thousand dollars of prime gifts, on the restaurant seats, including a great hand-knitted sweater for myself, some wonderful native carvings, and more importantly, some flimsy bedroom fashions for Shelley that I was anxious to see modeled. We were, after all, newlyweds. I wondered what it would take to convince the Captain to shut off the engines for a few minutes while

I went back for them.. The engines were roaring. There was no going back. Were we stoned out of our minds by a little brew of pot? Most definitely. What a way to end a wonderful vacation. And, by the way, Bruce now resides in one of our log homes.

Bruce knew what he wanted in his home. It first had to be comfortable and he'd been working on the plan for quite a while to accomplish that. All rooms led to an open living area for informal get-togethers with friends. Of course the massive granite stone fireplace became the focus of the room that contained the inviting soft leather couch and chairs. With the recycled pine floors and cherry kitchen cupboards, the kitchen glowed with a warm ambiance. There was a private den that opened onto a cozy sunroom and provided a great overview of the property which was great for hiking and bird-watching.

A nice reading nook that overlooked the fireplace below was not to be left out either. A dormer with a Palladian window added a bit of luxury to the upstairs loft bedroom. The bathroom spa, complete with whirlpool and soothing music, guaranteed relaxation. It was turning out, however, that the space could not include everything on Bruce's list. I suggested a small saltbox addition to the front, which gave an interesting line to the overall design besides giving him that extra needed room. I think the bachelor found the satisfaction he sought.

Bathroom Spa
Complete with whirlpool and soothing music, guaranteed relaxation.

Still reaching

for the sky

And standing high while looking over Ontario's fabulous Muskoka Lakes

I got a tip about a structure that might be a period log house, supposedly due to the depth of the door and window jambs. This was a good enough clue for me to jump in the Rover and drive out to Palmerston to check it out for myself.

I must say, I was somewhat surprised when I got there to see the later façade ripped off and the logs bared for easy inspection. They were the usual size of log, about fourteen inches wide and the usual thickness, almost always about eight inches. The real surprise though was that they weren't laying horizontally as you'd expect. They were standing up, as though reaching for the sky, the way they grew quite naturally. From bottom sill to plate log, they stood like soldiers, standing tight together as if in defense to an oncoming army.

I didn't know what to make of it at first, this being the strangest example of a log house I'd ever encountered... in Ontario I mean. It is a form of country architecture in Scandinavia, I know. There's no reason

immigrants from there could not be found here. And why wouldn't they build in a form they were familiar with — especially given the great pine timbers we were blessed with, the favorite wood of builders of log homes and woodworker craftsmen throughout North America.

The next thing I noticed was the unusual way the hand-hewn timber floor joists were carried into the log walls. They were actually mortised into the log posts (which they are now) and blind-pegged from both sides to hide within the depth of the upright chinks. It was obviously quite a job to get this house apart without damaging it. And we were realizing that we were being educated as we went about the job of taking it down. We thought we knew everything about building log houses — but we didn't. And we didn't have to jump a ship to Copenhagen to learn these tricks. By the time we got it back up we could add European artisans to our resumes... kind of.

Upright logs
Why not? If that's what you know, that's what you do, right? They did, whoever they were, and a good job too, that was for sure. It was a tough job undoing it.

Chinking
Vertical chinking was not something we'd encountered before. Thinking about it, it didn't seem too difficult. Maybe even easier. On second thought — maybe not.

When my client, the Fells showed us their site we were quite impressed. It was up at the north end of the Muskoka lakes near the town of Rosseau where we had just taken down a fabulous building on a huge piece of property overlooking the three lakes that formed the Muskokas. It was a log gambrel mansion called "Harmony Lodge" owned by Hiram Walker, the whiskey baron. Evidently, Royals slept there on occasion. William and Fergy, I think they were called. A developer wanted the site for his twenty-thousand-square-foot modern cottage. This whole area was the summer playground of rich and famous stars, whether movie, hockey or music.

The Fells site for instance, abutted Kurt and Goldie's choice of lot. Unfortunately, they were in LA making "Overboard" at the time, one of my favorite movies, so they missed seeing me. The site was a bit tricky to navigate since there was a tall granite wall outcrop about a foot (maybe it was a yard or two), from the foundation that insisted on staying where it was. We did get the frame up once again, ready for their carpenters to take over. I think if they had tried to cover up the logs a loose beam just might have accidentally fallen on them, like in the movies.

The ultimate antique

To complement the historic community of Queenston

It was kind of becoming a habit. I couldn't drive too fast through an area where I figured old homes lurked. Sometimes they were hidden by the modern buildup near the road. Other times you might see one peeking out from the overgrowth as if hoping to be found. Well, number two highway through Whitby was an early-founded area (witnessed by the once great Georgian home I just passed), neglected and looking pretty forlorn. But not far past it on my left I happened to notice something promising. It didn't give much away, that was for sure, but it was enough. Even though it was almost completely covered with weeds and bushes I could still make out its symmetrical front façade — a center door with a transom, and a door on each side of it. There was even a single sash left that was the giveaway, only the upper twelve-light sash but I was convinced.

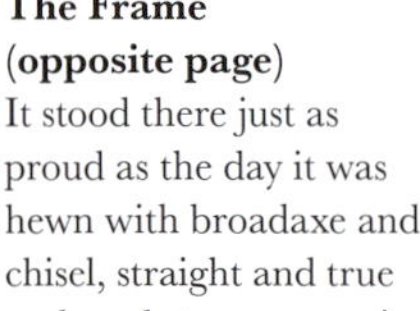

The Frame (opposite page)
It stood there just as proud as the day it was hewn with broadaxe and chisel, straight and true and ready to serve again.

This had to be an early 19th century home for sure. I pulled over and parked in the weeded driveway, probably the first to do so in years. No one had been taking care of this one. I spent an hour or so going through the place, which to my surprise, wasn't in as bad a shape as I supposed it to be. The fact that the back wing, set perpendicular to the front, was a full two stories, really surprised me. This was no small job, I realized.

It only took one afternoon to find the property owner, who happened to be E.P. Taylor, renowned owner of Canada's finest thoroughbred champions. I was to deal with his manager of the horse farm. I made an offer to remove the building for restoration. They had thought of tearing it down but after I explained our business, they were pleased to oblige me as long as I left the grounds clean of debris.

Our crew went through the laborious task of carefully removing every piece and numbering it for future rebuilding. The three-thousand square foot house took up a lot of storage space but I didn't expect to have it long. I had a few potential clients for it.

Of course it had an interesting history as most fine houses do. It was built in 1830 by a prosperous Pennsylvanian, Robert Schooley for his son Robert Schooley Jr. who hid from the British following his role in the unsuccessful Mackenzie Rebellion of 1837.

Bev and Doug Munkley saw my ad in *Century Home* magazine and came to check it out. They explained how they'd always been admirers of antiques and early houses. This new idea of restoring one seemed to have them captivated. They considered the idea of the house as one of acquiring "the ultimate antique." The couple seemed equally adept and capable of taking on the responsibility of managing the restoration.

"This house of 'Wilderness Georgian' design has a very symmetrical and ordered look about it with Greek Revival touches in the entry, plus heavy soffits and frieze on the outer trim," said Doug, "and the frieze has fourteen separate layers of wood to create the look." Doug, it seems, did not take long to know his house.

Portico
Not just beautiful but a handy place to sit and wait for the rain to stop.

The first thing however was to find the ideal property on which to rebuild. They wanted to find something as close as possible to Dr. Munkley's work as the Head of Emergency at St. Catharines Hospital.

Near Niagara-on-the-Lake they found a magnificent site overlooking Queenston Landing along the Niagara River. For a while in the 18th century, the area was the staging ground for everything that moved along the St. Lawrence River.

"We were very particular about making an accurate restoration while also making the home warm and livable. The fabulous location made the two work well into one. This being a labor of love for us, we intended to take our time. We were fortunate in that the home had only ever had three owners, so it's never been detrimentally renovated."

Because of all the historic homes in Niagara-on-the-Lake (some of which we had built), they were able to find tradesmen familiar with early cabinetry and framing. A mason who had worked on the restoration of Fort George was just one of the enlisted members of the crew. It was Doug as his own contractor, who would ensure the authenticity of every aspect of reconstruction as Bev researched and oversaw the decorating, including a full year of painting.

The further Doug and Bev got into the "package" of parts, the more they realized the daunting task at hand. A seemingly unaccountable number of beams, including four mantelpieces, doors, paneling, trim,

window frames and flooring had survived and were ready to be put back together. Only the kitchen floor was too worn to use. It turned out that the original windows had to be replaced. That was usually the case. I introduced them to my maker of vintage-style windows, the ones we'd been using for over thirty years, Mennonites in western Ontario, who were great to work with, once they were supplied with accurate details and sizes.

Watercolor (above)
A lovely watercolor of the house in winter by Bev's twin sister.

Chimney
Looking like a Roman ruin, the two story fireplace stands surveying the exterior for the first time in almost two centuries.

The basement was finished with original posts, beams and floorboards standing out proudly. When Bev and Doug realized they needed a large storage place, they had me design a twenty-four by thirty-six foot coach house prior to the move that doubled as a garage and skylit studio for Bev's work. The only other addition was the back sunroom and patio deck with a walkout from the second floor bedroom. I gave a nod to the architectural influence of Niagara-on-the-Lake, which overlooks the river, adding some classical grace to railings and a bit of the Greek Revival detail hinted at the front of the house.

All in all, I think it turned out even better than expected, certainly due to the gallant effort of Bev and Doug.

Majestic over Milton

Another historic home takes root on the Niagara Escarpment

We'd been given the tip where an old log house might be but we'd need a canoe to get to it. That was Okay with me. I'm as comfortable in a canoe as a chrysalis in a cocoon.

We came back a few days later and paddled across, saving miles of treacherous undergrowth and black flies. Northern Ontario could be a real challenge to navigate in the summer months. But we had to determine if the story was real. If so, some very hard work could be ahead. Steve and I pulled the canoe well up on shore and headed off in search of the rumored house. We hadn't trudged too far before I made out a derelict chimney above the tree line.

So it was true. The old trapper had lived there on the other side of the lake. We were told that he was long gone now though. But that too could be local hearsay.

I had to wonder if we'd be looking down the barrel of an old flintlock rifle. As we approached the venerable log walls, it did have the look of that era. I was pleased to see the nicely matched logs that explained the wide expanse of overgrown brush around the house. Obviously, every available tree nearby had been harvested, and pines too, my favorite species for warm, tight wall-building. Plus, the dovetailed corners were expertly done. I'm sure glad we pursued this one.

The door gave a loud creak as I pushed my way in. Great! The original floors were still intact, worn smooth from more than a century of use. An old pot-bellied stove stood in one corner. But there was no evidence of a fireplace or furniture for that matter. Maybe it ended up in the stove.

Free Fuel
Except for finding or felling it, carrying it, cutting it, stacking it, getting it in. Right. No cost at all.

I was surprised to find all of the windowpanes unbroken as well. This guy certainly took good care of the place. There was a bit of a crawl space under the floor that showed me the big sleepers, probably cedars responsible for carrying the house. There were remains of a few traps and some whiskey bottles under there. Somebody else had moved in. The nose knows. And not in the basement. No, these critters are fussy, living high on the hog. I gingerly made my way up the staircase to find strong evidence of the family that had left us a welcoming card. Well, that can be dealt with easily enough. A thorough spraywash will clean up those boards. The coons can find themselves some other digs. At least the porcupines hadn't been in to dine on the woodwork. I've lost many roof rafters and even parts of log walls to those guys.

So now what? Now we had to get some more help to disassemble the house in order to have it ready come winter. I rented a good-sized rowboat and motor for the crew and their gear. There'd be no crane to lift the logs down, that's for sure. No, this was manpower time. We'd set up a gin pole once the roof was off and use ropes and pulleys in the time-tested method of ages past. Once each wall was tagged and numbered, they'll be taken down and laid out in separate piles for transport.

Of course, I had a plan all along. It was just a matter of using what you've been given. This time it was the Canadian seasons. We inspect and plan in the summer, we collect in the winter.

That's when I gave the no-name lake a name, "Sleighbell Lake." I liked the sound of it. Yes, we were going to bring the logs out over the ice. We were going to sleigh them out with good strong horse teams, just like they might have been used in the old days.

Winter eventually came as usual for stage two to begin. Finding a farmer with horses was easy. He and his hearty sons were as excited as we were to do the job.

I think the sturdy ponies they hitched up were ready and willing too. For them it was a piece of cake. In fact, the whole operation looked like a fluffy white cake topping, the logs slipping and sliding along through the snow and over the ice like a big party game.

We put some sleighbells on our lead pony (we named him Rudy) who, by the way, did not have a red nose.

Once on the other side of the rink, the new game was on. The skid steers (mechanized) took over and loaded everything on the flatbeds for the trip back to the yard. Another great house was salvaged and will live again as a country home where it would be needed.

And it turned out it was needed in Milton. A couple named Dave and Ann Katz had a beautiful eleven-acre property on the escarpment that overlooked the city. It was a veritable forest of hardwoods on the hill with an eventual site for a home well down a new lane into the valley. I could see that if it was to go there, the trip to the road at the top could be a problem in the winter. But that was their choice and we began design plans.

The Room End
Rare as can be — an original room end in original paint that includes the firebox, the bake oven, a corner cupboard, a closet and even a dry sink.

Two log houses were to go into the design as they planned for a large family. The first one I showed them was about twenty-five by thirty and had wonderfully large logs. The other from Sleighbell Lake was slightly smaller. It seemed fitting that the two houses came from the Ottawa Valley and would be staying together. I suppose it was not an accident that the craftsmanship and the size of logs used were similar too. We decided the smaller one would be best used as the kitchen addition, the other being the main house with main staircase, living room and upstairs bedrooms. After a few weeks on the drawing board, the overall plan still wasn't as large as required however, given the rooms we were drawing up. I found a way to get the main house up to twenty-five by thirty-five by introducing six-foot wide stone fireplaces at the gable ends as well as a wide entrance at the front by adding sidelights. The bell-cast porch roof would disguise the cutline between the logs. Fortunately, the smaller addition was big enough to allow for a very large master bedroom.

Dave and Ann decided they'd need a garage that might later become a guesthouse. So,why not a nice little log house I also had in inventory. Done. They also took a shine to a rare form of fireplace wall that I had.

It was as if it had been waiting for them to find. It would be glorious on the gable end wall of the kitchen, comprising the bake oven beside the conventional hearth, as well as a dry sink at one end, all in the original red paint. And two great period mantelpieces, of course, would be used for the second and third fireplaces.

It took most of the season to put it all together and everyone was quite pleased with it. Anne called me back about every five years to see how the house had weathered. We rarely found much to touch up. It was only after forty years that it needed some chimney work, nothing too serious.

The art of craft and the craft of art

Showing off
their stuff on the Bluffs

Jane Fairburn and Mark Roger have entered my sphere many times over the years. Sometimes it may involve a visit to their ranch where a number of period buildings sat in various degrees of disrepair — but not beyond the scope of utility and even beauty, once attended to. One in particular, a log house of common size but ample potential, came alive again under the care and focus of Jane and Mark who managed a reputable restoration.

Or, another structure, perhaps one of early Ontario's stone houses, needed some work, or just an appraisal before they plunge into a project that just might be a pitfall.

There was one time when Highway 407 was being extended east on a route that promised an opportunity to acquire one of the many stone houses standing in its way. Together we joined up with others to inspect as many of them as we could fit in during the daylight available. Some of them had their own idiosyncrasies and charms and deserved careful scrutiny. Others did not demand attention, having been sorely neglected. There was one that Jane fell in love with, and I was not surprised. Of the eight or nine stone houses we saw that day, I too would have picked this one. It had wonderfully large granite stones and many period features you'd expect in an 1840 Georgian farmhouse; great paneled wainscoting, its original wide pine floors and even a staircase with the birdcage newel post, though sadly damaged by vandals. But there was enough quality there to have Mark make an offer to the powers that be. I thought it was a generous offer but was very surprised when it was ignored without an answer.

It wasn't long after that I noticed the house was gone. I found out that it had been bulldozed, the beautiful stones buried in the road foundation. Undeterred, Jane and Mark's hunt carried on, this time for a stone house on a large acreage that would promise some safety, not to mention, hopefully being in excellent condition. They eventually found it, a bit east of Peterborough and in very fine condition, recently restored on its

Mantle (opposite page)
Reigning over the room, a majestic mantelpiece in quartered oak with the customary tiles of the period.
H 66" W 96"

LET IT SNOW!

own private hundred acres. It even had a pond to the south, a few steps from the front entrance. This one seemed like a keeper. I was impressed with the job someone had done. Mark took on the task of fitting up the barn as well for weekend use. Another outbuilding was being restored on the property as an office, for which Jane requested assistance from me regarding replacement windows.

Then, when the idea dawned, of putting a few of my houses in a book (each with accompanying stories), I thought of their home on the Bluffs. It was a bit different than most of my projects, being in the Arts and Crafts style. They happened to catch me just as I'd inventoried quite a treasure trove of architectural artifacts of the period. They realized immediately the appropriateness of the windows, doors and mantelpieces for their house. I thought it would make a fine addition to the book collection. It turned out that each and every piece found a place, giving the house the authentic look it required. It was like the house had been waiting patiently for the missing pieces. Charlie Schlegel, my cabinetmaker on this one, did a remarkable job of interpreting and building the staircase I'd designed for the house. The slight turn under the ceiling for the railing (in a hardwood) was particularly difficult and was executed by a specialist.

Painting (opposite page)
A monumental landscape by Doris McCarthy, once a close neighbor and friend, who established the Artist-in-residence program at the base of the Scarborough Bluffs.

Glass
Since the middle ages stained glass has been the interface between art and architecture. When glass replaced mica and alabaster, light became the artist's partner. An art for eons. And here was the house that could use it. The craftsperson appeared, a master of her craft. Chris Montgomery's work enlivened the house immeasurably.

And Chris Montgomery did a fine job restoring some of the lead muntins for the doors as well as creating some fine stained glass pieces, a craft that she masters.

I always offered each of my former clients that are included in this book to offer the option of commenting on the project as they experienced it or to include some of the history that I'm sure I missed. Here is Jane and Mark's addition to the text.

Staircase
With tulips decorating the perforated stair slats, Charlie Schlegel displays his craftsmanship.

The Tulip
It was the Dutch who were dedicated to representing and popularizing the tulip in art that is often described as the flower that expresses a perfect love.

The Green Man
The pre-Christian symbol of the Green Man, as seen in several rooms of *Doire Naomh* represents the male God of rebirth and protector of "the wild" and the forest, reminding us of our intimate tie to the natural world.

DOIRE NAOMH

"Our home is situated near the highest point of the Scarborough Bluffs, some 200 feet over the waters' edge. Though we are only a half hour from the downtown of Canada's largest city, the overall feel of the property is something akin to what the ancients called 'Rus in Urbe,' or 'country in the city.'

The name of our property in the Scarborough Bluffs is Doire Naomh. Both in Scots Gaelic and in Irish, it translates to 'Sacred Grove.' The name is apt because our home rests at the foot of a mystical forest of beech and maple that descends down to the lake. A small creek ambles down the east side of the property. Large numbers of deer, coyotes, fox and rabbits also make this special place in the heart of the Bluffs their home, which contributes to an overall sense of enchantment.

Rather than being specifically designed, our home has evolved for close to 25 years — it is a place of solace and comfort that mirrors our collective experience both as a couple and as a family. We've been lucky to be in a home that does not attempt to compete with the beauty of the natural world that surrounds it.

In North America, it was translated into the American Prairie School by architects like Frank Lloyd Wright. Though our home reflects a mixture of influences, I see it primarily as an expression of the American Prairie School. Large windows that let in nature, a bungalow that is built into the forest behind natural forms that echo the natural world."

— Jane Fairburn and Mark Roger

If you want a golden rule that will fit everything, this is it: Have nothing in your houses that you do not know to be useful or believe to be beautiful.

— William Morris

You've reached Whitsend

Welcome to
our new beginning
at the end of
the road

Friends of mine were lucky to have come into a great house for sure, but more importantly, to have come into a wonderful marriage, the second for Christie and Bill. That is why this story is, in the main, a beautiful love story. Bill, a widower, is now on his own, save for family and their many friends. Christie, his love of 39 years, is now remembered in every glance though every room they shared in their early 19th century New Brunswick Raised Cape.

It was in the mid-nineties that I met the Whitmans in Lindsay at a sort of antiques show to which I had brought a few early artifacts to display. We had agreed to meet to discuss constructing a home on their 100 acre rural property. Bill said "We've been thinking of building a log house and want to make it look old." "Why pretend?" I countered. "Why not restore an antique home?" I showed them a photo of an Early Raised Cape that was located 30 miles from where Bill's father Tim had grown up on the rural eastern shore of Nova Scotia.

Christie, excited with her artist's eye, quickly saw the vision of the home's potential. Bill, initially somewhat skeptical, soon came around. They sent payment to the seller down east. Two days later I phoned the Whitman's saying, "This has never happened to me before. An American couple bought it out from under you."

Beauty
The shingled façade with its stand-out white trim looks good in every season, especially in nature's care.

I felt terrible. About five years later, Christie and Bill saw the home featured in an Early American Life magazine.

Tony Jenkins, a Kingston-based restoration builder colleague, flew to the Maritimes in his Cessna in search of another home. Kevin Harvey, a restoration builder in Nova Scotia, told Tony about a Raised Cape on the Petitcodiac River near Moncton, New Brunswick.

Tony created a video as he walked through this home that had not been lived in for years. The video showed torn wallpaper, broken glass and soggy mattresses on the floors, evidence of an abandoned house in distress. You would think this would put off most home buyers. Often it would, but it is best to show the dirty clothes that have to be dealt with. Further inspection by Tony revealed paneling of beautiful, wide bead-boarded walls in every room and "HL" hinges on all the doors. This was unheard of, something you'd only see in a museum village restoration.

Hinge
(opposite page, top)
New Brunswick, c. 1820,
Good old HL hinges,
beautiful to find and
easy to apply.

Boards
Early and original paint
and beaded for all walls
and even floors and
ceilings, rarely found in
this great condition.

Another feature noted, one that I had never seen before, was that the exterior sheathing boards were completely covered in birch-bark, obviously a deterrent against the Maritime wind and damp. The home was timber-framed of course, the timbers numbered with Roman numerals chiseled into the wood. This is something we often see in our log houses.

There were just too many interesting and unique aspects to the structure to miss the chance that a potential homeowner and this rare building could share a worthwhile future together. Christie and Bill were not about to miss this opportunity. Christie's parents, after seeing Tony's video, were unconvinced, exclaiming, "What are you two doing?"

Fortunately, Shirley Robinson, who was commissioned by the City of Moncton to paint a significant home in commemoration of the 100th anniversary of the City's incorporation, chose to paint this home before it was taken down and removed. Her painting shows later add-ons, a prominent dormer and a porch, which somewhat masked its beautiful simple lines. Known locally as the Steeves home, it was built by a close relative of William Steeves, New Brunswick Father of Confederation. Mrs. Robinson's painting occupies a prominent place in the William Steeves Museum home.

With the go-ahead, Kevin Harvey and his crew spent five weeks carefully disassembling the home. He then accompanied the disassembled home as it was driven by a French Acadian to the Whitman's Orillia, Ontario home. There he spent many weeks stripping wallpaper and layers of paint off the bead-boarded paneling. Careful to preserve the original colors of the boards, Kevin too realized that these early colors are only seen in museum village restorations and on some antique furniture that hadn't been over-painted.

Somehow Christie juggled her hospital job, her work on completing a Masters Degree in Psychology, and working along with Kevin and his brother on the house restoration at the Whitman's rural property. Bill cut back on his private psychotherapy practice hours so he too could work on the restoration.

Sheeting
Covering the post and beam framing with new pine boards, the house takes shape.

Fireplace
A simple, understated mantle surrounded by an early horizontal wainscot.

Happiness
Bill and Christie, the happy couple, soon after finishing the house.

Funding the project became a challenge, as banks are typically reluctant to fund rural, owner-built, antique home restorations. Fortunately, a psychologist friend of Bill had a high school friend who was a Canada Trust vice-president. Bill phoned him, and funding was quickly arranged.

A few minor changes to the interior were made during restoration. Two hallway walls were removed to expand the parlor/living room, and the master bedroom. William S. Hoar, historian, told the Whitman's that the original parlor was opened only for funerals, weddings and "Guests from the Boston States (i.e. New England)."

Christie and Bill moved into their home in March 1995, deeply grateful that they had chosen to go with the grueling yet intensely gratifying antique home restoration option.

For 13–14 years Christie and Bill hosted an annual Irish Traditional music weekend, during which fiddle and flute workshops were offered. 22–24 students, already accomplished musicians, some from the USA, attended. These Whitsend Irish Weekends became legendary.

Though comfortably settled in their home, Christie had one more project in mind: a long stone fence around their large yard. "Way too much work," Bill pleaded, to no avail. Scouring their acreage, searching for rocks with a dolly for many years, Bill finally completed Christie's stone fence.

The homeless

collector

After living like a gypsy for a year, I finally find a place for some antique treasures in a small apartment

Shaker Box
Hancock Massachusetts, 1927, an oval bandbox with four fingers made by Shaker Freida Sipple.
H 5" W 13" D 9"

I've lived in a few nice homes. I even had to build some since I've always been quite particular about my environment. Being the slave of beauty could account for it. Perhaps that's why I've titled this book, "A Dedication to Beauty."

Fortunately, I've taken pictures along the way so they could be included in this book which, by the way, has been a labor of love for me because I love these houses, each and every one. Roseville, Brandon Manor and Cavan were lived in happily for assorted years each, with two wives for assorted years each. The loss of a home or wife came with the hurt you may expect, given the changing challenges and unexpected occurrences that somehow govern us.

Few these days can realize that in the eighties a twenty-two percent mortgage was not uncommon. The worst of those times maybe having to give up Roseville too soon after building the stone studio that was my finest architectural dream realized. I was not the only one disappointed, as many friends had enjoyed the particularly charming space it offered for creativity.

Each of those three homes were distinctly different, but their uniqueness perhaps was the charm that carried them to fruition. The first of log, the next a post and beam classic and the other a reproduction to emulate the 18th century which has always fascinated me. Needless to say, they accepted antiques quite naturally, I thought, as though anywhere else they would feel out of place.

Antiques have interested me since my teens. My eyes never tired of seeing them as being major players in my sight line. Of course, one soon learns that one cannot consider real ownership of such things. To appreciate them is the gift of them. We sometimes have to part with them in order to carry on.

Sister Frieda
Sister Hulings was not lazy; she worked six days a week. She enjoyed dairy and kitchen work and did chores willingly. "I did not always do them right or well," she recalled, "and when this happened I was simply told to do them over again. There was no yelling or nagging. To do a thing right was considered only reasonable and logical," and so except for the knitting, she learned to do all things right. Into old age, she remembers Sister Freida's (above) advice, "All that you do, do with all your might."

Spice Box
A thirteen-drawer spice box, Connecticut, mid-19th century, original blue and red paint found at the Bowmanville Antique Show.
H 19" W 21" D 10"

RENOVATION
WORLD

Quebec Armoire
Early 19th century, original dark green paint, with eight panels of roundels.
H 54" W 45" D 16"

Glazed Cupboard (opposite page)
Harrowsmith, Ontario, mid-19th century, tan with light brown panels over original dark green, cornice with gouge carving and reeded door trim.
H 85" W 54" D 20"

Log Cabin Quilt (above)
Ontario, c. 1870, light and dark blue, light and dark tan and orange, representing the hearth of a log cabin.
H 80" D 68"

The parting with favorites is just part of the end game. There were some sad times when beautiful objects, those fond companions of mine, left my company to adorn other homes. That does not, however, stop the true collector from searching for replacements. "The turning point" in the experience of antique collector is a gradual recognition for many and an eureka moment for a few... as was mine, one workday in the shop.

As a foreword I will add some context. It was the early seventies that I found a particular disappointment at what was becoming too popular for my liking. Collectors were stripping their furniture finds. I found out myself by almost falling into the same fad, the same trap, that of removing late overcoats of paint, no matter what color, to reveal the beauty of the wood beneath, whether it be pine, maple or another species of wood.

So there I stood, in front of a large two-tier dish dresser from Markham, all of sixty-five dollars dished out. I had the pot of paint stripper in my hand, about to begin. I suddenly realized how beautiful it was. I imagined it looking at me, as if thinking, "what is that fool going to do to me?"

Was it that thought that brought me to my senses? The dresser had been wearing its lovely dressing of rich burgundy color, most likely since it was built about one-hundred years or more ago.

I was dumbfounded. I put the pot aside, only picking it up again if it was needed to carefully remove an unimportant color to arrive at an original one, usually a beautiful one, hidden beneath. This then, was the true history of the piece brought into the light. The colors that I found chosen back then constantly amazed me, particularly when you arranged the pieces in a room where they played off each other. The rooms came alive, so much more interesting than a room of cleaned wood surfaces, ubiquitous in their common display.

Now I should add that the aforementioned pertains in the main to country furnishings. There will always be that fine league of antique furniture built in the hardwoods (i.e. walnut, birch, tiger maples, etc.), that stand on their own merit of classic form, craftsmanship, and finish that can't be compared to any other.

Miniature Wall Shelf
Port Hope, Ontario, last quarter of 19th century, with three compartments for little treasures.
H 8" W 8" D 4"

Document Box (opposite page)
Maine, c. 1850, with original red and yellow paint and brass escutcheon.
H 4" W 10" D 5"

Cupboard (opposite page)
New York State, c. 1840, pine with beaded back boards, original gray/blue exterior with pumpkin interior.
H 74" W 41" D 17"

Our antique shop of two rooms stood adjacent to our log home. We started to keep it filled with new discoveries — a table with a red skirt and legs, a food locker in a faded gray-green, an overpainted black Windsor chair, taken down to its original blue, and so on. Gradually, other like-minded collectors found us and kept our stock moving. I had to scour the countryside, even venturing into the United States to find such pieces.

Oh yes, by the way, after enjoying the burgundy dresser for many years, it found a new home... for well upwards of ten grand. So if it's beautiful, leave it alone. It could pay off in more ways than one.

I started collecting burl bowls, commonly a fine category of treen (the early name for woodenware), in the early seventies. I was intrigued by their history and exceptional craftsmanship. I guess it was my visit to Devere Card, now considered to be the King of Treen, that hooked me.

Frank N. Magill, Editor

My antique world was about to erupt forever. He took a chair to watch my eyes widen with the excellence I saw that lay everywhere. In one corner was a stack of burl bowls nested in each other. The bottom ones were about two feet or more in circumference. At the top of the four-foot high pile was a tiny five-inch beauty sitting comfortably. I knew a little about these hand-carved Indian bowls. Most were hewn from white ash, an incredible feat considering the tools available at the time. Looking further, I noticed also, trenchers, spoons, salts and various drinking vessels, all in gorgeous burl. This was obviously an incredible collection that must have taken Mr. Card a lifetime to amass. I asked if I could pick up a piece, a particularly fine bowl, off-round, being carved rather than turned. I fell in love with its distinctive grain. It had a silky feel that needs centuries to acquire.

Ash Burl Ladle
Northeastern woodlands, native-carved, late 18th to early 19th century.
Length 13" Bowl 6"

Pantry Box (below)
Ontario, last half 19th century, with exceptional five-pointed stars.
H 2" D 6"

I had heard that it was the Indians who used burl before the coming of those newly arrived settlers and taught newcomers its use. Although only a small percentage of American treen was ever made from burl because of natural limitations of occurrence and availability, burl is both eminently suitable for certain purposes and a very beautiful material. The greatest hazard to woodenware was splitting. The convoluted and interlaced grain structure of burl resists splitting to a marked degree, furnishing a turned or hewn utensil which was not subject to splitting along one axis line. For this reason burl was a superior material for the making of treen. It is highly probable that many small articles of burl have been saved far past their period of normal use because they were made of pretty wood and have survived to the present.

I didn't want to overstay Mr. Card's welcome. I thanked him for the honor of seeing his collection but not without taking at least one item of

Oval Splint Box
Quebec, late 18th century, original red, blue-green and black paint, with rosettes and geometric forms.
H 7" W13" D 9"

burl home from The King of Treen. My collection of burl has grown in the apartment, being small acquisitions. They didn't take up much space, especially when neatly nested one inside the other.

I had to give up the idea for my fourth personal house, another of log in the country. I realized I was not up to the task, my knees giving up on me, the consequence of having been a parachuting teenager who thought himself indestructible. So here I am now, in an experience I never accounted for, apartment bound. Not that I'm not grateful. I should have thought of it earlier and saved myself some of the aggravation that home-ownership deals to oneself.

I lived for a year like a gypsy, having little luck finding a space for myself, Blondie, my very large labradoodle, and knees that cannot navigate stairs. And that's not to mention, my diminished collection of antiques. It wasn't too difficult to find homes for the bulk of the furniture. One client alone took about half of the contents that resided in my nine-room Georgian home to fill space in the huge log home we built for her.

Burl Bowls
(preceding page)
A nest of eight beautiful burl bowls take up little space on a table top.

Gameboards
(preceding page)
A collection of four Parcheesi games. Shown not to scale — approx. 20" sq.

Burl Handled Bowl
(this page)
New England, c. 1800, Abenaki Atlantc white cedar with eight scribed geometrics and a human effigy.
L 9" Bowl 5" D 5"

Saltbox
Prince Edward County, Ontario, c. 1810, forged nail construction, original brown paint.
H 13" W 14.5" D 5.5"

Splint Box
(opposite page)
Quebec, c. 1800, birchbark with red stain, compass-scribed decoration and faded history on lid, early French wallpapered interior.
H 5.5" W 11.5" D 8"

Finding this apartment in Cobourg was a godsend. Though only about eight-hundred square feet, it's amazing how much I could squeeze into the four rooms. Large pieces wouldn't fit so it left me to collect smalls, including more burl treen of course.

As shown in the preceding double page spread, burl bowls of various sizes can very neatly be stacked inside each other, only taking up the space of the largest of them on a table or atop an armoire. It is one of the tricks that allows the collector to continue to collect. I suppose that at some point, there will be no space left. Do I miss living in the country? Yes I do. At least I get to it often enough as I help site a client's home on their chosen property, the likes of which our great Ontario provides in abundance for all. I sometimes get to visit the houses of friends I've made while working for them. It has been a very rewarding experience and I am proud of the legacy I've left in the interest of history and the beauty and satisfaction that home ownership can be.

THE WINCHESTER BOOK
THE WINCHESTER BOOK - Madis
1 of 1000
Masterpieces of World Philosophy

Here's a few more of the houses that I've had the pleasure

▲ A fabulous barn frame from Puslinch becomes a designer's dream in Niagara-on-the-Lake.

▲ A stone house in Peterborough needed a fenestration fix upgrade.

▲ A classic Georgian brick saved from its western Ontario location to a new spot just north of Cobourg.

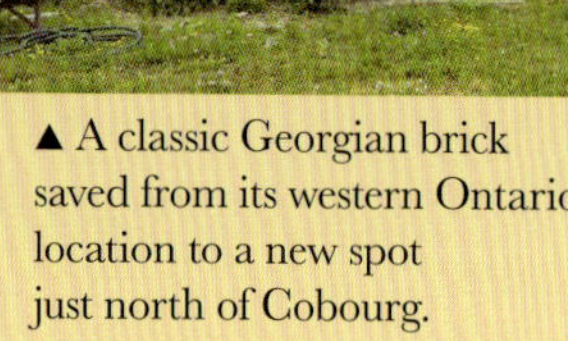

▲ Another stone house almost beyond help, until we saved it for future generations.

▲ One of the best two-story log houses we ever found. From Roseville, Ontario.

A barn frame from Morganston, used for the skeleton of this house now in Cobourg. ▼

of being involved with over the years. They *all* have stories.

▲ To save the original interior of this house, we decided to move it whole from Barrie to Acton.

▲ A stone house in north Toronto that needed the period interior it used to have.

▲ A stone classic on Lake Scugog that needed a matching addition.

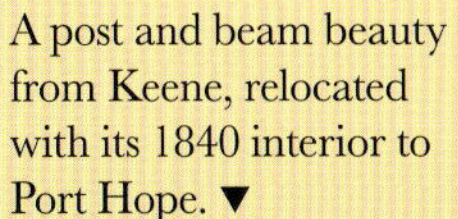

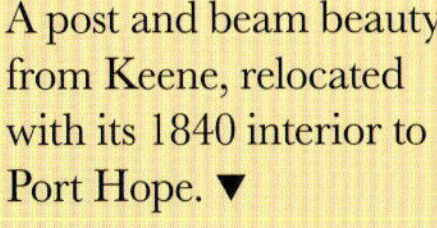

A post and beam beauty from Keene, relocated with its 1840 interior to Port Hope. ▼

A 30 x 40 two-story with a log cabin kitchen. ▼

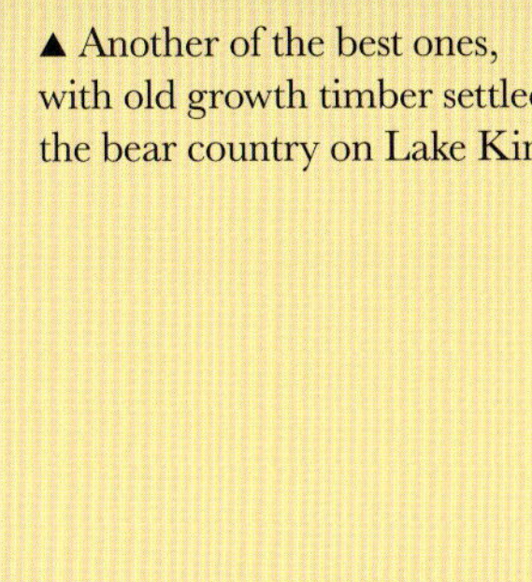

▲ Another of the best ones, with old growth timber settled in the bear country on Lake Kinnisis.

Special mention and many thanks
to friend, collaborator,
fellow collector, and technological wizard,
Ken Burgin,
without whom this book
may not have appeared.

Also by the author

From the Caterra Series:

Book One–The Stradivaripuss Job

Book Two–The Chinese Catnip Caper

Book Three–The Pharaoh's Wand

Book Four–The Lost Professor

Book Five–The Case of the Upside-Down Milk Torture

Book Six–The Crystal Cat Skull

Book Seven –The Case of the Golden Arrow

Book Eight–The Race to the Moon

Book Nine–The Séance Sting

Other Books:

Reflextions in the Face of Oblivion

A Silent Space

The April Antiques and Folk Art Show

In Production:

Smile of a Word — Cry of a Story
volumes one, two, & three

The Captain of Night

I Am a Snail

I Am A. Nightmare

Endangered

The team over the years

Bill Beaton
Brian Clutterbuck
Case Jensen
Charles Shanks
Charlie Schlegel
Christine Ferreri
Dave Kennedy
Dave Wales
Dieter Sebastian
Don Beamish
Doug Vickers
Ed Moseanko
Eugene Power
Glen Ward
Grant Eskerod
Jeff Cooper
Jim Tedford
Joe Sica
John Bartram
John Riddle
John Wittenbols
Kevin Harvey
Les Brittan
Maarten Bomers
Marc Howell
Mike Loudfoot
Paul Currie
Paul Harper
Peter Huffman
Phil Powers
Reverend Ken
Richard Gautier
Rick Washbrook
Rob Keyes
Rubin Lacey
Sandy Thaine
Sarah Barnard
Sean Espinoza
Tim Krahn
Tony Jenkins
Washboard Hank
Wayne Nickolas

All with a craft or other to contribute in major and/or minor ways
...and all of those clients who personally put their heart and sweat into the job.

Business associates and friends of the arts that have offered inspiration

Aaron and Ivan Weber, Betty Sterling, Bill and Joanne Patterson, Bill and Paula Lishman, Bill Dobson, Bill Mason, Blake and Ruth McKendry, Bob and Mavis Perkins, Bruce Chambers, Clay and Carol Benson, Chris Edgar, David Field, Dennis Raleigh, Devere Card, Dick Lloyd, Don Friary, Don Olson, Fred Savard, Gabriel Lachappelle, Howard Pain, Jane Roberts, Jim and Kathryn Calladine, Joanne Getz, John Fleming, John Luke, John Rogers, Joseph Goden, Keith Marlowe, Ken Burgin, Ken Ross, Larry Foster, Linda Rosen, Lyn and Merla McMurray, Marlene Hilton-Moore, Michael Rowan, Myrtle and Percy Catchpole, Peter Baker, Peter Eaton, Piet and Lynne Van Schydel, Ralph and Patricia Price, Ray Smith, Rob and Nancy Lambert, Robert Avery Smith, Rod and Aggie Brook, Roger Bacon, Ron Myers, Smitty Axtell , Steve Powers, Vic Snow, Wendy Hamilton

Book reference

Arthur, Eric, and Whitney, Dudley,
The Barn – A Vanishing Landmark of North America,
McClelland and Stewart Limited, 1972

Baker, Peter E.,
Celebrating Canada – Decorating with History in a Contemporary Home,
Dundurn Toronto, 2017

Benson, Ted, *The Timber Frame Home,* The Taunton Press, 1988

Burgin, Ken, *Real Stories About Ersatz Antiques,* 2022

Card, Devere A., *The American Hearth,*
Broome County Historical Society

Card, Devere A., *The Use of Burl in America,*
Munson-Williams-Proctor Institute, 1971

Chamberlain, Samuel, *Open House in New England,*
Bonanza Books, 1937

Cruikshank, Tom, and Stokes, Peter,
The Settler's Dream – A Pictorial History of Buildings of Prince Edward County,
The Corporation of the County of Prince Edward, 1984

Cruikshank, Tom, *Old Ontario Houses – Traditions in Local Architecture,*
Firefly Books Ltd., 2000

Dobson, Henry, and Barbara,
The Early Furniture of Ontario and the Atlantic Provinces,
M F Feheley, 1974

Duncan, David Douglas, *The Silent Studio,*
W. W. Norton & Company, 1976

Duvall, Lesley, and Duane, Sharon, *In the Shaker Tradition,*
Koomler, Friedman/Fairfax, 2002

Endersby, Elric, and Greenwood, Alexander, and Larkin, David,
Barn – The Art of a Working Building,
Houghton Mifflin, 1992

Ewing, Douglas C.,
Pleasing the Spirits – A Catalogue of a Collection of American Indian Art,
Ghylen Press, 1982

Finley, Gerald, *In Praise of Older Buildings,*
Frontenac Historic Foundation, 1976

Fleming, John A., and Rowan, Michael J., *Folk Furniture,*
The University of Alberta Press, 2004

Fleming, John A., *The Painted Furniture of French Canada 1700 – 1840,*
Camden House and Canadian Museum of Civilization

Hale, Jonathan,
The Old Way of Seeing – How Architecture Lost its Magic (and how to get it back),
Houghton Mifflin Company, 1994

Hodgins, Eric, *Mr. Blandings Builds His Dream House,*
Simon and Schuster, 1946

Hutchins, Nigel, *Restoring Wooden Houses,*
Firefly Books, 1999

Isham, Norman M., and Brown, Albert F., *Early Connecticut Houses,*
Dover Books on Architecture, 1965

Kettel, Russell Hawes, *The Pine Furniture of Early New England,*
Dover Publications Inc., 1965

Kirk, Malcom, *Silent Spaces – The Last of the Great Aisled Barns,*
Bullfinch Press, 1994

Ladd, Paul R., *Early American Fireplaces,*
Hastings House, 1977

Larkin, David, *Country Wisdom,*
Houghton Mifflin Company Limited, 1997

MacRae, Marion, and Adamson, Anthony, *The Ancestral Roof,*
Clarke Irwin and Company Limited, 1963

Mayer, Barbara, *In the Arts and Crafts Style,*
A Running Heads Book, 1993

McRaven, Charles, *Building the Hewn Log House,*
Thomas Y. Crowell, 1978

Mercer, Eric,
Furniture 700 – 1700 The Social History of the Decorative Arts,
Meredith Press, 1969

Mohr, Nancy L., *The Log Home – Classic Log Cabins of North America,*
Running Press, 2001

Nutting, Wallace, *Furniture Treasury,*
Macmillan Company, 1928

Pain, Howard, *The Heritage of Upper Canadian Furniture,*
Van Nostrand Reinhold Ltd., 1978

Palardy, Jean, *The Early Furniture of French Canada,*
Macmillan of Canada, 1965

Parkman, Francis, *Pioneers of France in the New World,*
George N. Morang & Company, 1900

Pinto, Edward H.,
TREEN and Other Wooden Bygones – An Encyclopaedia and Social History,
London: G. Bell & Sons, 1969

Powers, Steven S., *North American Burl Treen,*
Mercantile/Image Press, 2005

Primary Wood-Using Industries in Ontario,
Ministry of Natural Resources, 1983

Pye, David, *The Nature and Aesthetics of Design,*
Barrie and Jenkins, 1978

Rempel, John I.,
Building with Wood and other aspects of nineteenth-century building in Ontario,
University of Toronto Press, 1972

Shackleton, Philip, *The Furniture of Old Ontario,*
Macmillan of Canada, 1973

Simons, T. Ralph, *Feng Shui Step-by-Step,*
CreateSpace Independent Publishing Platform

Smith, Nancy A.,
Intimate Treatises of the Architecture of the American Colonies and the Early Republic, Old Furniture – Understanding the Craftsman's Art,
Bobbs-Merrill

Symons, Scott, *A Romantic Look at Early Canadian Furniture,*
New York Graphic Society Limited, 1971

Vrest, Orton, *The Forgotten Art of Building a Good Fireplace,*
Yankee Press, 1965

Whitehead, Russell F., *The White Pine Series of Architectural Monographs,*
Marchbanks Press, 1917

Wilson, P. Roy, *The Beautiful Houses of Quebec,*
University of Toronto Press, 1975

"If you wisely invest in beauty,
it will remain with you all the rest of your life."

Frank Lloyd Wright